Kestrel skeleton

White-bellied
sea eagle

Verreaux's eagle

European kestrel

EYEWITNESS GUIDES

Common, or crested, caracara

EAGLE

Written by
JEMIMA PARRY-JONES
The National Birds of Prey Centre

Photographed by
FRANK GREENAWAY

Saker falcon

Bald eagle

DORLING KINDERSLEY
London • New York • Stuttgart

African hawk eagle

Peregrine falcon

DK

A DORLING KINDERSLEY BOOK

Project editor David Pickering
Art editor Kati Poynor
Assistant editor Julie Ferris
Managing editor Gill Denton
Managing art editor Julia Harris
Production Charlotte Traill
Picture research Rachel Leach
DTP designer Nicola Studdart
Consultant Colin Shawyer

This Eyewitness ® Guide has been conceived by
Dorling Kindersley Limited and Editions Gallimard

First published in Great Britain in 1997
by Dorling Kindersley Limited,
9 Henrietta Street, London WC2E 8PS

A CIP catalogue record for this book is
available from the British Library.

ISBN 0 7513 6105 4

Colour reproduction by
Colourscan, Singapore
Printed in Singapore by Toppan

Egyptian vulture

Foot of wedge-tailed eagle

White-backed vulture

African harrier hawk

Contents

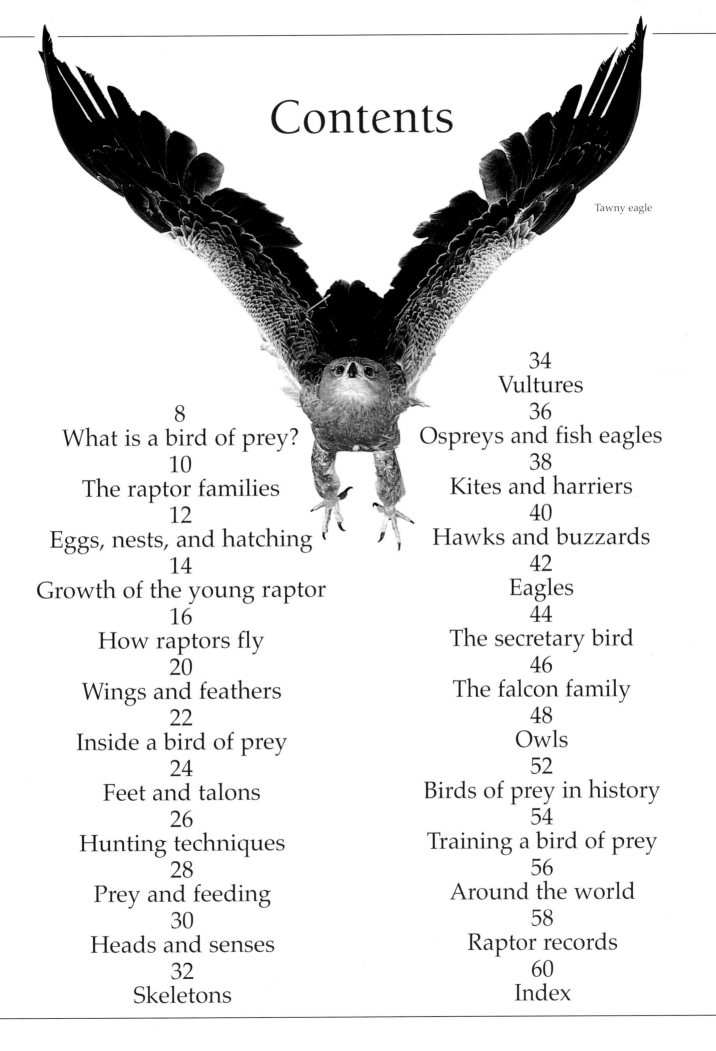

Tawny eagle

What is a bird of prey?

BIRDS OF PREY are not the only birds that hunt for their food, nor the only birds that eat meat, or have hooked beaks, or fly very well, but they are the only birds that combine all these characteristics, and with them, one very distinctive feature: they kill with their feet. They are called raptors, from the Latin *raptare*, "to seize, or grasp" because they seize their prey in their feet. Their lethal talons can snatch fish from the water, strike birds out of the air, and rip open animal quarry (prey). Like lions and tigers, raptors are "top predators": they hunt other creatures, but nothing hunts them, except for other raptors – and humans.

SPECIAL DIET
Some raptors will eat just about anything, others are specialists. One of the most specialized of all is the snail kite of Florida in the United States. It lives on a diet of water snails. Its beak has a long, curved hook with which to remove the snail from its shell.

Primary feathers, like tail, are fanned out for landing

Tail used for steering, soaring, and braking

Large vultures have powerful beaks, to rip open the carcasses of large animals

The feet of vultures, such as these white-backed vultures, are weak because they don't need to kill their prey

CATCH IT WHEN IT'S DEAD
There is a major exception to the rule that birds of prey hunt their food: vultures. Vultures are specialized in scavenging, that is, finding dead animals, rather than hunting live ones. Other raptors will eat carrion (dead flesh) if they happen to come across it, but only vultures are carrion specialists. Most vultures spend much of their time soaring high in the sky, scanning a wide area for signs of death.

SYMBOL AND STANDARD
Many peoples have taken birds of prey as symbols of what they most revere: gods, freedom, the sun, royalty. Many nations, kings, and armies have taken birds of prey as their emblems. This eagle standard comes from the French army, c.1800.

Ravens eat meat in much the same way as many birds of prey

CARNIVOROUS BIRDS
Many meat-eating birds are not birds of prey. For example, magpies hunt and kill small birds. Ravens such as these, which belong to the crow family, have a similar diet to that of buzzards. They have strong, pointed beaks with which they kill young rabbits, and even the occasional lamb. But only raptors kill with their feet.

Wing feathers fan out to give extra lift (pp. 16–17)

BORN TO KILL
Birds of prey are perfect hunters. The tawny eagle pictured here is a superb flier, and has the characteristic lethal raptor feet. Its curved beak acts as a knife and fork for tearing through flesh and eating its prey. Raptors' skill as hunters can work against them if the environment becomes polluted: if each animal they eat contains a tiny amount of pollutant, they end up taking in a large amount. So environmental damage often hurts them first.

Female merlins are usually one-third heavier than males; this is average for falcons

In some birds of prey, the male is much more colourful than the female

Killing feet: powerful with huge, curved talons for grasping prey

DOES SIZE MATTER?
Birds of prey are unusual in that the females are usually bigger than the males. (Scientists call this "reverse sexual dimorphism".) The size difference varies. It is greatest in sparrowhawks, where the female is twice the size of the male. Vultures are one of the exceptions: males and females are usually the same size, and male condors are larger than female condors.

The raptor families

THERE ARE RAPTORS on every continent except Antarctica: over 300 species of diurnal (day-flying) bird of prey, and about 130 species of owl. Each of these species plays its own unique part in the ecosystem. Scientists class all the day-flying birds of prey together in the "order" (group) *falconiformes*, which contains five separate "families". The owls have their own order, the *strigiformes*. Scientists give each order, family, and species a Latin name. The local names for each bird are different in different countries, but the Latin name is always the same, so that scientists, and others, do not become confused. The Latin names of the birds in this book are in the index on p. 60.

Black vulture flying; vultures soar to look out for dead animals

The powerful king vulture; New World vultures, like storks, urinate on their own legs to keep cool

OSPREY
Ospreys form a one-species family: they are unique and cannot be classed with anything else. Specialists at catching fish (the only raptors that dive deeply into the water), they eat very little else. They are "cosmopolitan", that is, found world-wide, where there are shallow waters – lakes, rivers, or coastal areas.

Pandionidae
osprey

osprey

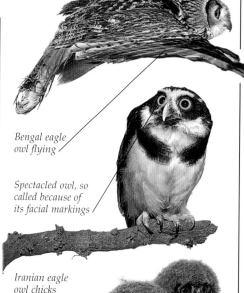

Bengal eagle owl flying

Spectacled owl, so called because of its facial markings

Iranian eagle owl chicks

NEW WORLD VULTURES
These vultures live in the Americas. They occupy the niche in the food-chain that the Old World vultures fill in the rest of the world: eating up carrion. Although they look quite similar to other vultures, they are, in fact, more closely related to storks than to any other raptors and so, according to recent scientific research, should no longer be classed in the *falconiformes* order. There are seven species of New World vulture.

Andean condor, largest of all raptors

SECRETARY BIRD
Secretary birds, found in Africa, are another unique species, in a family of their own. They have much longer legs than other raptors, stand 1.2 m (4 ft) tall, and hunt by walking, not flying, across grasslands, and stamping on the prey they find.

OWLS – RAPTORS OF THE NIGHT
Owls are not related to the diurnal birds of prey. Most are nocturnal (hunt at night) or crepuscular (hunt at dawn and dusk). Their sight is excellent, especially at night, and their hearing is phenomenal. They fly silently, hunting by stealth, not speed. There are two families: the dozen or so species of barn owl (p. 49), and the rest.

The turkey vulture is the only raptor known to smell out its food

Sagittariidae
secretary bird

secretary bird

Strigiformes
owls

owl

Cathartidae
New World vultures

condor

Falcons, such as this lanner falcon, have distinctive long, pointed wings

American kestrels (right) and other kestrels are very good at hovering

Large falcons, such as this peregrine, are the fastest birds on earth when they dive down on prey

Caracaras are the only falconids to build nests and to hunt on the ground

Foot of Verreaux's eagle from Africa

Large accipitrids have massively powerful feet

Eagles, such as this bald eagle, can see at least twice as far as humans

Hooked tip of beak rips into flesh; sides of the beak cut it off

Bald eagles' broad wings enable them to soar effortlessly

The African harrier hawk is halfway between a harrier and a hawk

Egyptian vulture shows the broad, muscular accipitrid tongue

ACCIPITRIDS
These are much the largest group of raptors: there are 237 species. Hawks, eagles, buzzards, kites, Old World vultures, and harriers are all accipitrids. Their kinship shows in their similar eggs, tongues, and moulting patterns. They all build nests. They kill with their feet (falconids often use their beaks as well as their feet), and they squirt out their droppings – falconids let them fall. Most accipitrids have a protective ridge of bone above the eye.

THE FALCONID FAMILY
There are three main groups of falcons: the true falcons (which include kestrels), the little-known forest falcons, and the pygmy falcons, or falconets, smallest of the raptors. The caracaras of the Americas are also related to them, and form part of the *falconidae* family, which contains about 60 different species, found all around the world.

Falconidae
falcons and caracaras

kestrel

Accipitridae
hawks, kites, buzzards, eagles, harriers, Old World vultures

goshawk   *kite*   *buzzard*   *golden eagle*

Eggs, nests, and hatching

AT THE START of the breeding season, the male birds try to show the females that they will be good mates. Males perform display flights, then bring the females food to prove that they will be able to feed a family. The pair bond is formed, and the new pairs build nests. Pairs often defend a territory around their nest to protect their food supply. A few species, however, including several of the kites and vultures, breed in colonies. The smallest birds of prey brood (sit on) their eggs for 28 days before they hatch, the largest for 54 days. Usually, the females brood the eggs. The males bring the females food until the new chicks are big enough to be safely left alone.

Bald eagle egg

Ural owl egg

Peregrine falcon egg

African pygmy falcon egg

ALL SORTS AND SIZES
The above eggs (shown actual size) illustrate the variety of raptor eggs. Owl eggs are much rounder than those of day-flying raptors. Condors and large vultures lay only one egg at each breeding attempt, most eagles two or three, small birds, like kestrels, about six, a few species, such as snowy owls, up to 14.

STARTING A FAMILY
Usually, males and females build their nests together. Male goshawks, however, build three or four nests, by themselves, for females to choose from. Nests are often built up trees or on cliff ledges – in any safe place. Only a few raptors, such as harriers and caracaras, normally build nests on the ground.

Buzzard eggs in buzzard nest

ONLY THE STRONG SURVIVE
Some eagles have two chicks, but usually only one survives. If food runs short, the older kills the younger. In a few eagles, the older always kills the younger. The chicks of smaller raptors do not usually attack each other, although they do compete for food. If food is scarce, the weakest will die.

In Verreaux's eagles, the first chick hatched always kills the second, even if there is plenty of food for both

Larger branches are lodged in treetrunk first, then twigs, then leaves

12

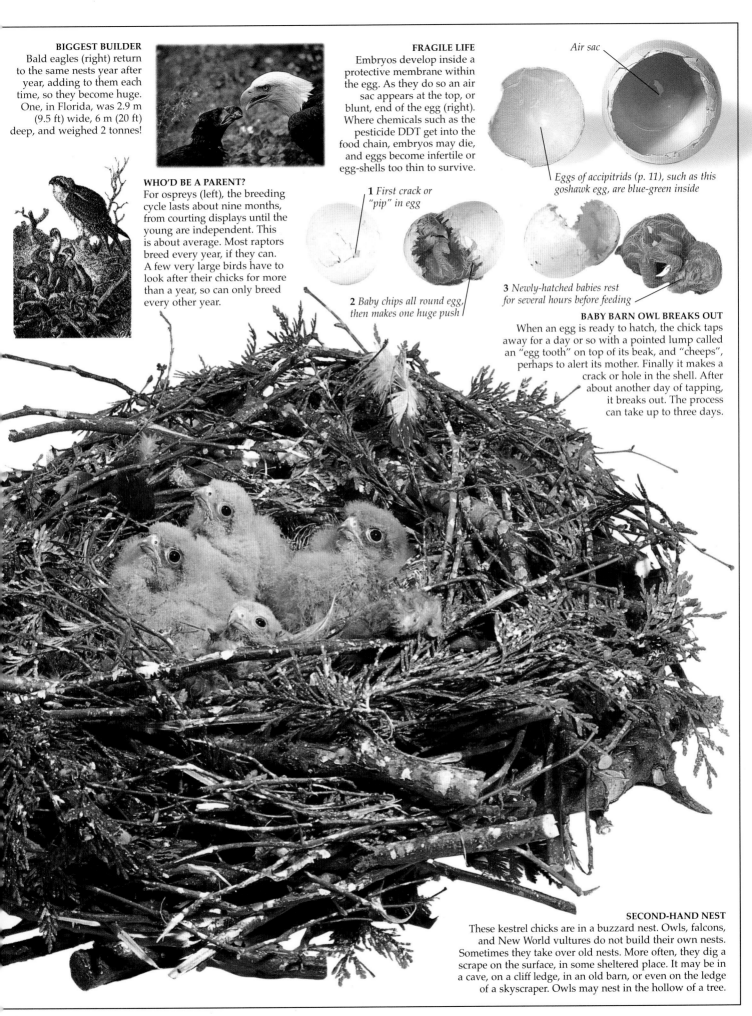

BIGGEST BUILDER
Bald eagles (right) return to the same nests year after year, adding to them each time, so they become huge. One, in Florida, was 2.9 m (9.5 ft) wide, 6 m (20 ft) deep, and weighed 2 tonnes!

WHO'D BE A PARENT?
For ospreys (left), the breeding cycle lasts about nine months, from courting displays until the young are independent. This is about average. Most raptors breed every year, if they can. A few very large birds have to look after their chicks for more than a year, so can only breed every other year.

FRAGILE LIFE
Embryos develop inside a protective membrane within the egg. As they do so an air sac appears at the top, or blunt, end of the egg (right). Where chemicals such as the pesticide DDT get into the food chain, embryos may die, and eggs become infertile or egg-shells too thin to survive.

Air sac

Eggs of accipitrids (p. 11), such as this goshawk egg, are blue-green inside

1 *First crack or "pip" in egg*

2 *Baby chips all round egg, then makes one huge push*

3 *Newly-hatched babies rest for several hours before feeding*

BABY BARN OWL BREAKS OUT
When an egg is ready to hatch, the chick taps away for a day or so with a pointed lump called an "egg tooth" on top of its beak, and "cheeps", perhaps to alert its mother. Finally it makes a crack or hole in the shell. After about another day of tapping, it breaks out. The process can take up to three days.

SECOND-HAND NEST
These kestrel chicks are in a buzzard nest. Owls, falcons, and New World vultures do not build their own nests. Sometimes they take over old nests. More often, they dig a scrape on the surface, in some sheltered place. It may be in a cave, on a cliff ledge, in an old barn, or even on the ledge of a skyscraper. Owls may nest in the hollow of a tree.

Growth of the young raptor

Two-day-old black vulture chick

YOUNG BIRDS OF PREY grow very fast, racing through the most vulnerable stage of life. For their first few weeks they just eat, sleep, and grow. Young sparrowhawks are fledged (full-grown and flying) after 26 days, and can hunt well enough to feed themselves four weeks later. Larger birds develop more slowly, but even a golden eagle is fledged at two and a half months and independent of its parents three months later. In temperate climates, raptors need to be full-grown and ready to hunt before winter arrives and food becomes scarce. Only a few very large birds in hot countries, such as martial eagles and Andean condors, grow more slowly.

2 weeks

3 weeks

6 weeks

8 weeks

10 weeks

4 At two weeks old this barn owl chick is eight times heavier than it was at hatching. Then (p. 13) it weighed about 12–14 g (0.5 oz). At two weeks it weighs over 100 g (3.5 oz).

5 The chick is nearly ready to stand up. It spent its first weeks sitting on its ankles. It is covered in thicker down, called secondary down, and can keep warm without mother.

6 The feathers are pushing through the skin, and the facial disc is beginning to appear.

7 Close to being fully feathered, it practises jumping and wing flapping in the nest to strengthen its muscles. It will be able to fly in about a week.

8 It is now fully grown and learning to hunt. It will still rely on its parents for a few weeks more as it learns to hunt well enough to feed itself.

Unlike many birds, raptor chicks (except for owls) have some vision at birth and can take meat from their mother's beak

"Egg tooth" (p. 13)

1 2-DAY-OLD PEREGRINE
At two days, all young birds of prey rely on the warmth of their mothers to survive. They eat meat from day one. Their parents rip it up for them until they can rip it up themselves. In a few species, parents regurgitate food for their chicks.

Chicks beg for food, cheeping and raising opened mouths to their parents

2 12-DAY-OLD PEREGRINE
At 12 days peregrines start to get a thick white down which means they can "thermo-regulate" – keep themselves warm without the heat from their mother. She can then hunt, with the male, to feed their rapidly-growing appetites. They can eat half their own body weight and more in a day.

Down inadequate to keep chick warm

Juveniles stay near the nest while their parents still feed them, then disperse

Juvenile colouration often has a buff edging

3 7-WEEK-OLD PEREGRINE
This seven-week-old peregrine is nearly full grown. Once it has fledged it will be called a juvenile, until it gets its adult plumage. It must then quickly learn to hunt well, or starve. Perhaps 50% of young raptors die in their first year (this varies with food availability from year to year). In temperate climates, many die in their first winter.

4 JUVENILE PEREGRINE
Most young birds of prey are a different colour from their parents. This allows them to hunt in the territory of adult breeding pairs, who would drive out other adults but leave juveniles alone because they are no threat until they are fully adult and ready to breed.

Beak will become strong enough to tear meat after a few weeks

Adults lose the buff edging to the body feathers and become all grey on the shoulders

Young peregrines (this one is one year old) usually have vertical bars or stripes

Horizontal bars and stripes replace the vertical ones of youth

5 ADULT PEREGRINE
Some birds, like kestrels, breed before they are a year old, if nest sites and mates are available. Others, like peregrines, start at three or four. Very large birds may not breed until they are six or seven years old. Birds that are over a year old but still in juvenile plumage are called sub-adults.

Characteristic owl ear hole: a long, thin slit

WHAT AN EARFUL
Owls have bigger ears than other raptors (p. 51), visible in this two-day-old owl chick. Like most raptors, they rip up food for chicks. A few birds of prey, such as vultures and snake eagles, regurgitate it – snake eaglets pull still-writhing snakes from their parents' mouths.

Feet very soft and weak at this stage; chicks spend their first few weeks sitting on their ankles

How raptors fly

AEROPLANES NEED an engine to push them forward; their wings will only keep them up. Raptors' wings provide both the power to go forward and the "lift" to stay up in the air. As birds flap their wings, the inner part of the wing provides most of the lift, the outer part most of the power. The flight feathers (p. 21) are specially shaped to improve the airflow over the wings, and thus the birds' flying ability. The tail is used for steering and for braking: it moves continuously as the bird steers through different air currents. The feathers fan out for a fast turn and open out completely as the bird slows to a stop. The various wing-shapes of different raptors enable the birds of each species to fly in a way that suits the terrain in which they live, and to hunt effectively.

The rounder wing of the true hawk or accipiter

FOREST FLYING
The hawk family (pp. 40–41) have a longer tail for their body size than most raptors. It helps them to turn fast and to stop quickly. Their short, rounded wings give them a fast takeoff speed. This is vital to enable them to catch prey before it reaches cover in the wooded areas in which they live.

Sparrowhawk

The primary feathers raised in takeoff position

The tail is raised to help with getting airborne

Legs take a while to be drawn up out of the way

Tail closed when bird is flying in a straight line, opened and tilted when turning

Powerful legs give great assistance with thrusting the bird forward and upward

The power comes from the breast muscles

KING OF THE FALCONS
The arctic gyr falcon is the largest and possibly the fastest of all the falcons (p. 58). Falcons have long, pointed wings which are not particularly good for soaring or gliding, although they can and do soar, but are perfect for fast flying. The narrowness of the wing reduces drag in the air, but also makes them less able to manoeuvre well, so they are suited to hunting in open country, rather than wooded areas.

The pointed wings of the falcon family

JUST HANGING AROUND

Eagles, such as this black eagle, are designed for soaring. They are not able to keep up flapping flight for long, and use warm air currents to lift them up, sometimes thousands of feet high, as they watch for prey. It is the raptor version of going up in a lift. Most big eagles and vultures live either in mountains and along coastlines, where there are lots of updrafts to soar on, or in hot countries with plenty of thermals (p.18).

Tail fans out to increase lift when bird is soaring

Outer primaries have to be very flexible

Inner primaries bearing the load

The covert feathers protect the bone which is very near the surface of the wing

The alula fits in here when not in use

Alula is raised when bird is slowing to a stop

TAWNY EAGLE TAKEOFF

During takeoff, a bird's wings are raised first and the legs push the bird off in a jump. As the bird jumps, the first downbeat happens. It is called the power stroke: the wings move forward and downward, giving the bird lift and forward motion. The primary feathers along the outer part of the wing (pp. 20–21) do most of the work on each downstroke, continuing to give lift and forward direction. On the upstroke, the primary feathers open to move upward more easily, and the secondary feathers on the inner wing maintain the lift.

LAZY FLYER

Condors' wings are huge, both long and wide, so the birds can soar for hours on rising air currents, looking for dead animals. But they cannot take off easily if full of food, or if they are somewhere flat. On flat ground, they have to do a running takeoff to gain speed before trying to get airborne. In their mountain homes, however, they simply open their wings as they take off from the ledges on which they live, and the updrafts do the rest.

Large wing area enables condor to glide on air currents rather than use the more tiring flapping flight

Large birds use the legs and feet as air brakes also

BRAKING ALULA

This red-tailed buzzard is in the landing position: its body is almost vertical to the ground, rather than horizontal as it is when flying. The wing and tail feathers fan out to slow the bird right down. At the top of the wings you can see two "thumbs" standing up. These are the alulas or "false wings". All birds have them. They smooth out the air flow above the wings at low speeds, and prevent the birds from stalling. The flaps, or slats, on aeroplane wings do the same job, but not so well.

Styles of flight

All raptors have one of three basic wing shapes. Falcons have slim, pointed wings, suited to sustained high-speed flight. Hawks, forest eagles, and other forest birds have short, rounded wings, which enable them to take off quickly and accelerate rapidly, but make fast, sustained flight too tiring. Vultures and other large raptors have long, rounded wings. These enable them to soar very easily on rising air, but cannot be flapped as quickly as the shorter wings of hawks and falcons, so the large raptors are not as fast or as agile.

Diving down to link toes

Once the feet are grasped the birds tumble towards the earth

Bald eagle will turn upside down to meet the other bird's feet

GRASP YOUR PARTNER BY THE CLAW
Some birds have very spectacular mating flights. Bald eagles fly really high and then, grabbing the feet of their new mate to be, they spiral downwards, falling together, then release one another. Some observers suggest that this flight is also to drive off unwanted eagles from the new pair's territory, so that they are not around to compete for food when the pair are feeding their chicks.

VERTICAL TAKEOFF
Caracaras are related to the falcons but don't have their fast flight. They are, however, much more agile in the air and on the ground. They can even fly vertically off the ground for several feet. This may be to catch insects they disturb while scratching through rotten wood. They spend much of their time on the ground scavenging.

Wings stretched back, moving the bird directly upwards

After pushing the caracara upwards the legs dangle rather untidily

Birds often circle by ridges, hoping to pick up a thermal

Bird reaching top of thermal; thermals only last up to a certain height

Raptors often glide from thermal to thermal, travelling without tiring

Thermals form readily over land, but not over water, so most raptors avoid flying over large expanses of water

UPWARDLY MOBILE BIRD OF PREY
The most important aids for soaring birds are thermals. A thermal is a column of warm, rising air. Thermals happen as the ground heats up during the day. Raptors can rise effortlessly in thermals, which are vital for migration (p. 56), as well as soaring, because they save the birds so much energy. Apart from thermals, raptors' other main sources of rising air currents are coastlines and mountain ridges.

*Wings beating fast, tail
starting to fan out as
the bird starts to hover*

*Kestrels have special, very
flexible necks that keep
their heads still, although
their bodies move slightly*

*The primaries
take the strain*

*Wing out in the
upwards climb*

ROLLERCOASTER LIFE
Raptors looking for a mate often do a beautiful
undulating flight to impress prospective
partners. They fly high, fold their wings and
drop like a stone, open the wings, pulling out
of the dive, climb, then close them again in
another dive. The display can also tell other
birds that the displaying bird has claimed the
territory over which it flies, and will guard it.

HELICOPTER BIRD
Kestrels specialize in
hovering as they hunt.
A few other raptors, such
as buzzards and snowy owls,
also hover occasionally. They use
the wind to assist them, flying slowly into
the wind so that their speed and the wind's speed
cancel each other out. Hovering enables them to
stay still and look out for prey over open country
where there are no perches on which to sit.

*Machine sketched by Leonardo da
Vinci, one of the earliest attempts
to invent a flying machine*

IMPOSSIBLE DREAM
People have always longed to fly like
birds but, even if we could make bird-
like wings for ourselves, human muscles
are far too weak for flight, unlike the
muscles of birds (pp. 22–23). On one
estimate, we would have to have chest
muscles 2 m (6 ft) deep for us to fly.

*Some kestrels, such as
this European kestrel,
have longer tails for their
size than other falcons do*

*Head thrust forward
in landing position*

*Primaries splayed out
and tilted for landing*

*Wider secondaries
still providing enough
lift to stay airbourne*

*Landing gear
ready for approach*

TAWNY LANDING
Often when a bird is
landing it will drop below
the perch on which it intends
to land, and glide up to it. When
they land from above the perch, birds
have to put on all the brakes: their tails fan wide
open, their legs are thrown forward, and their feet are
raised. Their wings are fanned out as brakes and their
heads drop so that they can see where they are landing.

*The centre two tail
feathers, called
"deck" feathers*

Wings and feathers

Birds are the only animals with feathers. Feathers serve two purposes. They allow the bird to fly and keep it warm. They are made of keratin, the same fibrous protein as the scales on reptiles, and hair and nails on mammals. A bird has a variety of different feathers. Most of the visible feathers are contour feathers. The larger ones are flight feathers, found in the wings and tail. Underneath are the soft down feathers which keep the bird warm. Other feathers have unusual, specialized functions: filoplumes act like eyelashes, semiplumes like a cat's whiskers, and bristles help with preening (caring for the rest of the feathers).

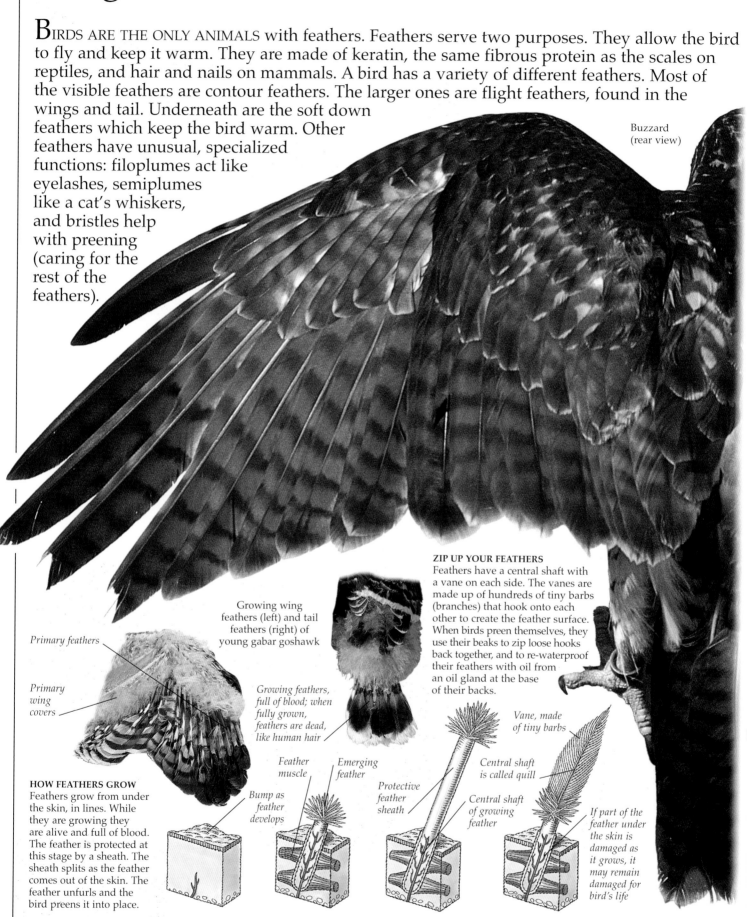

Buzzard (rear view)

Growing wing feathers (left) and tail feathers (right) of young gabar goshawk

Primary feathers

Primary wing covers

Growing feathers, full of blood; when fully grown, feathers are dead, like human hair

HOW FEATHERS GROW
Feathers grow from under the skin, in lines. While they are growing they are alive and full of blood. The feather is protected at this stage by a sheath. The sheath splits as the feather comes out of the skin. The feather unfurls and the bird preens it into place.

ZIP UP YOUR FEATHERS
Feathers have a central shaft with a vane on each side. The vanes are made up of hundreds of tiny barbs (branches) that hook onto each other to create the feather surface. When birds preen themselves, they use their beaks to zip loose hooks back together, and to re-waterproof their feathers with oil from an oil gland at the base of their backs.

Feather muscle

Bump as feather develops

Emerging feather

Protective feather sheath

Central shaft of growing feather

Central shaft is called quill

Vane, made of tiny barbs

If part of the feather under the skin is damaged as it grows, it may remain damaged for bird's life

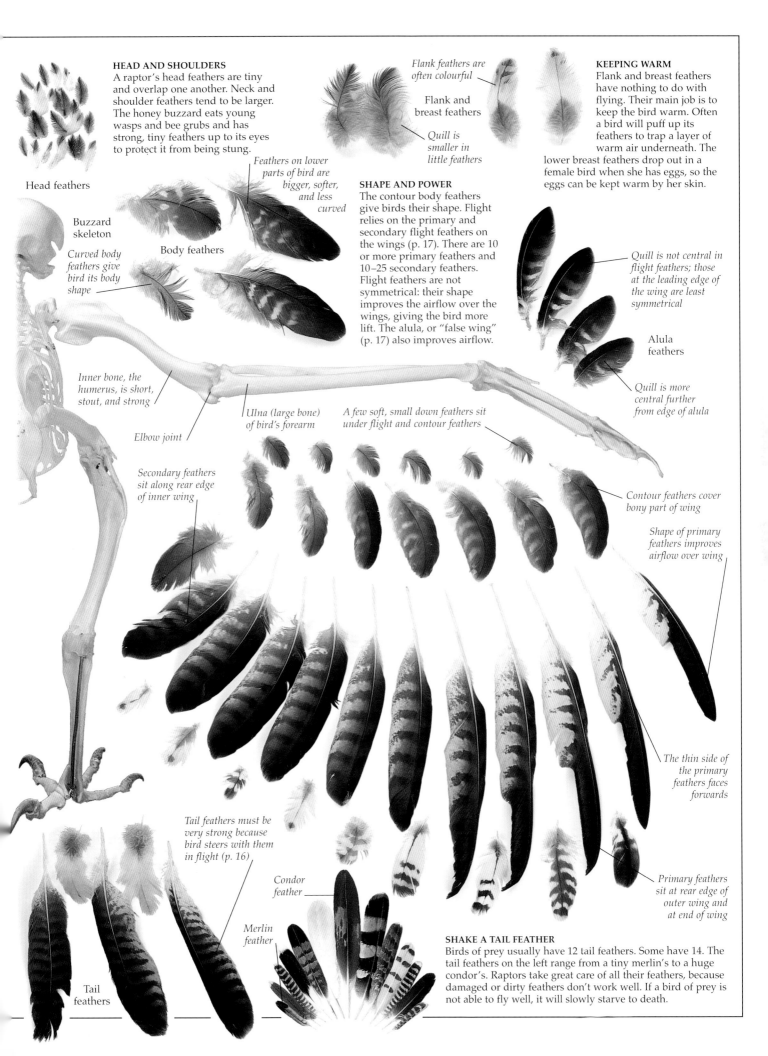

HEAD AND SHOULDERS
A raptor's head feathers are tiny and overlap one another. Neck and shoulder feathers tend to be larger. The honey buzzard eats young wasps and bee grubs and has strong, tiny feathers up to its eyes to protect it from being stung.

Head feathers

Buzzard skeleton

Curved body feathers give bird its body shape

Body feathers

Feathers on lower parts of bird are bigger, softer, and less curved

Flank feathers are often colourful

Flank and breast feathers

Quill is smaller in little feathers

KEEPING WARM
Flank and breast feathers have nothing to do with flying. Their main job is to keep the bird warm. Often a bird will puff up its feathers to trap a layer of warm air underneath. The lower breast feathers drop out in a female bird when she has eggs, so the eggs can be kept warm by her skin.

SHAPE AND POWER
The contour body feathers give birds their shape. Flight relies on the primary and secondary flight feathers on the wings (p. 17). There are 10 or more primary feathers and 10–25 secondary feathers. Flight feathers are not symmetrical: their shape improves the airflow over the wings, giving the bird more lift. The alula, or "false wing" (p. 17) also improves airflow.

Quill is not central in flight feathers; those at the leading edge of the wing are least symmetrical

Alula feathers

Quill is more central further from edge of alula

Inner bone, the humerus, is short, stout, and strong

Elbow joint

Ulna (large bone) of bird's forearm

A few soft, small down feathers sit under flight and contour feathers

Secondary feathers sit along rear edge of inner wing

Contour feathers cover bony part of wing

Shape of primary feathers improves airflow over wing

The thin side of the primary feathers faces forwards

Tail feathers must be very strong because bird steers with them in flight (p. 16)

Condor feather

Merlin feather

Tail feathers

Primary feathers sit at rear edge of outer wing and at end of wing

SHAKE A TAIL FEATHER
Birds of prey usually have 12 tail feathers. Some have 14. The tail feathers on the left range from a tiny merlin's to a huge condor's. Raptors take great care of all their feathers, because damaged or dirty feathers don't work well. If a bird of prey is not able to fly well, it will slowly starve to death.

Inside a bird of prey

UNDERNEATH THE FEATHERS, raptors have powerful muscles. Under the muscles is the skeleton. Protected within the skeleton are the internal organs, which enable the bird to breathe, to breed, and to draw out the nutrition from its food. Birds have an incredibly efficient respiratory (breathing) system to supply the oxygen they need when they fly. Their digestive organs are capable of dissolving fur, feathers, small bones, and whole insects. The totally indigestible parts of prey are coughed back up as pellets. Because they use up energy so fast, the smaller species can starve very quickly, and need lots of food to keep up their body temperature, especially in cold weather.

Strong but light skull

Neck has 14 vertebrae, allowing bird to twist head right round and look in every direction without moving body

Inner wing bone (humerus), very strong because all the chest muscles that move the wing are attached to it

Breastbone (sternum) is very deep and strong to anchor the chest muscles

On this model, wing muscles are exaggerated for extra visibility

Final vertebrae are fused together to provide a strong support for the tail

Golden eagle skeleton

Powerful toes to crush and kill

Eyes are so large that raptors cannot move eyeball within eye socket; flexible neck compensates

Esophagus: long, thin tube of muscle

Crop: food is stored here; bird does not have to digest it all at once, so can eat much without indigestion

The "hand and wrist" bones are fused together

Massive breast muscles give power for flight

The "finger" bones

Birds of prey have highly developed leg muscles

Raptors' feathers usually conceal the fact that they have long legs

THE COOL WAY TO BREATHE
When birds fly, their muscles work so hard that they need to take in huge amounts of oxygen and to lose heat very fast. Their breathing system enables them to do both. It is far more efficient than ours. Inside the skeleton, as well as two lungs, is a system of air sacs running through the body. These air sacs enable the bird to pull in lots of oxygen very fast. At the same time, the air passing rapidly through the air sacs cools the bird down.

Bones of spine are largely fused, so there is little muscle needed along back

Weight is concentrated around centre of gravity

Posture of model is slightly unnatural

Side view of
golden eagle's
muscles

A PELLET A DAY
All birds of prey produce pellets of
undigested material, such as this,
every day or so. Scientists use these
pellets to find out what birds have
been eating. Owl pellets (p. 50) are
the most revealing because their
stomachs are less good at digesting
small bones than are the stomachs
of diurnal (day-flying) raptors.

*Falcons and other
day-flying raptors
digest most of the
small bones of their prey*

Falcon
pellet

DIGESTION TIME
When birds of prey eat, the meat goes into the crop
first, except in owls, which do not have a crop.
Then it goes into the stomach where the
unwanted parts, such as feathers, are
packed into a ball to be regurgitated
the next day, and the rest is digested.

Golden eagle model
showing muscles (left)

Golden eagle (right)

THE ULTIMATE CHEST
Nearly half the weight of a bird
of prey is taken up by its muscles.
The breast, or pectoral, muscles
are the largest. They do the work
of making the bird fly. Because
the big flight muscles are all in
the chest, the wings are kept
light and the weight of the
bird is kept central, making
it more stable in the air.
The leg muscles are
also very powerful, to
grip and crush quarry.

Feet and talons

TALONS AND TOES
Talons, which would be toenails on our feet, can be huge on large eagles. In some female eagles, the inner and back talons can be as long as your thumb.

A RAPTOR'S MOST IMPORTANT TOOLS ARE ITS FEET. Their size, shape, and strength show what it is capable of catching. For example, kites can be large birds – red kites are about the size of a small eagle – but their tiny feet only allow them to catch frogs, beetles, and half-grown rabbits. The peregrine, on the other hand, is smaller than the kite but has enormous feet, enabling it to catch birds almost its own size. Vultures have weak feet, because dead animals don't struggle very much, whereas the martial eagle of Africa can catch and kill young ostriches and small antelopes! If you want to know what a bird of prey eats, look at its feet.

Feathers fanned out for landing

This bone is the foot bone, although it appears to be part of the leg

GOLDEN EAGLE FOOT
Birds, like dogs, walk on their toes. The bird "foot" has become an extension of the leg. It helps to absorb the shock of landing and to push up when taking off. The ankle is halfway up the leg. The knee is hidden under the feathers at the top of the leg.

Falcons' feet are large but not very strong

These bones are the toes, and the talons are the toenails

SAKER FALCON FOOT
Falcons often strike their prey at high speed, so that the force of the impact disables or kills the prey. They even occasionally close the foot into a fist and punch the quarry. They don't usually kill with sheer crushing power and may finish off their prey with their beaks, not their feet.

BLACK EAGLE
The African black eagle, or Verreaux's eagle, has enormous feet because it catches the nearest living relative of the elephant! It is a much smaller relative. In fact, the rock hyrax looks like a giant guinea pig. The eagle's big, powerful feet are ideal for grabbing these very stout, rounded animals.

BLACK VULTURE FOOT
The New World vultures have feet more like a big chicken's than a bird of prey's. These feet have very little grip or power, but are great for standing on all day. The feet of Old World vultures are more powerful, but still relatively weak for raptors of their size.

Soft feathering on owls' feet and legs helps to keep them warm and silent

Vultures' talons do not need to be curved, because they are used for walking not for killing prey

OWL FOOT
Most owls except the fishing owls have feathered toes to help with silent flying and landing. Owls, and ospreys, have a reversible outer toe. This toe sits forward when they relax, but is swung back when they grip something, to help them to grasp their prey, or perches, better. The rest of the birds of prey perch and grasp with three toes forward and one back.

When owls' feet are relaxed, they have three toes forward, one back

AFRICAN FISH EAGLE FOOT
The osprey and all the fish eagles have very scaly feet so that when they grasp a slippery fish they can hold on to it. The bottoms of their legs are bare, not feathered, so they don't have to fly around with wet feet.

SPARROWHAWK LEG
Sparrowhawks tend to catch small birds, such as sparrows, hence their name. They often snatch birds from the air. They have long, thin legs and toes, with needle-like talons, perfect for grasping their small, elusive prey. Raptors which catch more powerful prey, such as rabbits and other sizeable mammals, have relatively shorter, stronger leg bones.

The knee joint

The ankle joint

Talons more curved than other eagles'

Long, thin bones give extra reach

Birds perch and walk on their toes, not their feet

This foot is larger than a human hand

25

Hunting techniques

Eagle eating
a snake

MANY OPEN-COUNTRY RAPTORS hunt by flying high, surveying a wide area, then swooping fast. Eagles glide down quickly to take prey on the ground; falcons dive even faster to catch birds in mid-air. Harriers hunt differently: they fly low and slow, looking and listening for quarry in the undergrowth. Owls tend to do this too. Many raptors, especially those that live in wooded areas, or towns, will often "still hunt", that is, hunt from perches, sprinting out from cover when prey comes round the corner. Some, goshawks for example, fly close to the ground, using hedges and trees as cover, to surprise prey. A few birds of prey, such as secretary birds and caracaras, hunt on the ground, flushing out prey as they walk along.

STILL HUNTING
Buzzards, such as this red-tailed buzzard, are very good at still hunting. A buzzard will sit and watch and wait as a rabbit wanders, until that rabbit strays just too far from its hole, which is its last mistake. Birds such as kestrels that normally hunt in flight may still hunt when they have no chicks to feed, or are tired, because still hunting uses less energy.

Nictitating membrane (p. 30) often sweeps across to protect eye as bird attacks

The perch must be inconspicuous; many raptors have a favourite perch that they use frequently

Some raptors flit from perch to perch as they hunt (p. 40)

Feet can lock onto prey so powerfully that sometimes raptors find it hard to release prey

DROPPING IN FOR A BITE
Some birds of prey, like this red-tailed buzzard, will catch anything they come across. The red-tailed buzzard, or red-tailed hawk as it is called in North America, will hunt for small prey like this chipmunk, but can also manage a fully grown rabbit that weighs as much as the buzzard does. Other raptors, such as the snail kite (p. 8), eat one particular prey. Individual birds may develop their own specialities: some peregrine falcons wait on cliff ledges to ambush birds flying past.

Tail is spread out to act as a brake

FISHING EAGLES
Ospreys, fishing buzzards, fishing owls, and fish eagles, like this white-bellied fish eagle, live near sea, lakes, and rivers and catch fish. Except for ospreys, whose hunting technique is all their own (p. 36), these birds usually sit on a high perch watching the water for fishes feeding on the surface. A low-angle dive allows them to throw their feet into the water and snatch a fish.

Primary feathers fanned out to keep bird from stalling as it brakes rapidly

Hawks spot potential prey

One hawk swoops down to flush the prey out of cover

Other hawks move into position to ambush prey

Eagle surveys wide areas as it spirals high on thermals (p. 18)

VIEW TO A KILL
Large eagles (except forest eagles, p. 42) need wide, open spaces to fly and manoeuvre in as they hunt. They often soar, looking for tiny movements such as a rabbit flicking an ear or a hare scratching its side, and then stoop with deadly intent. At other times they may hunt from perches.

Eagle drops down on its quarry

STOOP TO CONQUER
All large falcons live in open country. There is no cover, so their prey can see them far away, and they may face a long chase to catch it. To help them get extra speed they climb high and stoop (dive) on their quarry, when it is far from cover. If they miss, they climb and stoop again.

Quarry driven into open

ALL IN THE FAMILY
Most raptors are solitary hunters. Sometimes breeding pairs hunt together. A few species work in teams. Harris' hawks hunt in family groups of up to six. Several birds may tackle the prey at once. If the prey is in cover, one or more birds may try to flush (frighten) it into the open. Occasionally the birds take turns to harass and tire prey, until it is confused, exhausted, and helpless. Together the group can tackle larger prey than one bird could on its own, such as jackrabbits twice as heavy as the largest Harris' hawk.

The kill

Prey and feeding

SOME RAPTORS WILL EAT ANYTHING, others are specialist feeders. The snail kite (p. 8) only eats snails, and the bearded vulture (left), eats mostly bones and marrow (the nutritious substance inside bones). Insects are very important to many birds of prey: 12 species eat only insects, 44 species eat mostly insects, and another 100 species occasionally eat insects. A few birds of prey even eat fruit as well as meat, such as the palm nut vulture, which is named after its favourite food. The small, insect-eating birds must eat their tiny prey frequently, but many of the larger birds survive on one or two kills a day, and can spend the rest of their time sitting and digesting. Vultures may have to look for a long time for food, so they gorge themselves when they can: a 5 kg (11 lb) griffon vulture can eat nearly 2 kg (4.5 lb) in one meal. Most birds of prey feed alone or with their families, but vultures and kites will gather in large groups at a sizeable food source, such as a dead buffalo or a rubbish dump.

BEARDED WONDER
Bearded vultures are named for the beard-like feather tufts on their faces. They eat bones. Small bones they swallow whole, large bones they drop onto rocks from about 60 m (200 ft), sometimes more than 20 times, until they break.

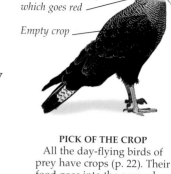

When caracara is upset or excited, blood rushes to skin above beak, which goes red

Empty crop

PICK OF THE CROP
All the day-flying birds of prey have crops (p. 22). Their food goes into the crop when they eat and is digested later. As they eat, the crop gradually bulges out. In most raptors, the crop is hidden by feathers, but in caracaras it is bare, and looks very odd when full.

Primary feathers are black, rest of bird is white

Black vultures can draw the feathers on their necks up when they are cold, or down when they are feeding, so they don't get blood over them

Vultures brace themselves on their strong legs to rip off tougher pieces to eat

BRING A FRIEND
It is thought that if black vultures such as these find a carcass whose skin is too tough for them to tear open, they will go and find a larger king vulture and lead it to the carcass. The king vulture rips it open and feeds, and the black vultures can eat too.

Skin above beak is usually yellow

Full crop; contrast empty crop of caracara on left

Caracaras scavenge dead rabbits, and most other things they find

NOT WELCOME AT THE FEAST
Some raptors, such as this Cooper's hawk, "mantle" their food. That is, they spread their wings out above it as they eat, hiding it because many creatures, including other raptors, might try to steal it. Raptors usually carry prey away to a safe place to eat it, if it is small enough to lift.

Wings outspread to hide food look like a cloak or mantle, so the action of spreading them to hide food is called "mantling"

Cooper's hawks eat small mammals and birds, such as this quail

Egg-shaped stones are preferred for throwing at ostrich eggs

SEASONS OF PLENTY
Each year, the bald eagles of North America's Pacific coast have a huge banquet as the salmon come upriver, lay their eggs, and die (p. 37). Other raptors benefit from occasional surges in the numbers of their prey, such as locust and mice plagues. Snowy owls and rough-legged buzzards lay more eggs in years when their main prey, lemmings, have a population explosion. The letter-winged kite of arid inland Australia does not breed until the rains are good and its main prey, the long-haired rat, is abundant; then it raises several broods one after the other.

Nostril, or nares, not see-through in Egyptian and other Old World vultures, unlike New World vultures (p. 31)

Pacific salmon die after they have spawned (laid their eggs) so the bald eagles just have to drag their bodies out of the river

BIRD-BRAIN EXTRAORDINAIRE
Various raptors eat eggs if they find them, but Egyptian vultures are the only birds that use a tool to do so, and the only birds of prey known to use a tool at all. To break into an ostrich egg, they pick up small rocks and throw them at the egg until it breaks open. Smaller eggs they pick up and throw at the ground. In South Africa, where ostriches are farmed commercially, ostrich farmers shot and poisoned Egyptian vultures; none breed there any more. Other ingenious raptors include bearded vultures. As well as dropping bones from a height, they also drop tortoises to break open their shells.

Ostrich eggs are the largest eggs in the world

Heads and senses

HUNTING OTHER ANIMALS is the hardest way to find your food. To help them, birds of prey have excellent eyesight – at least two or three times as good as ours. In one test, a buzzard saw small grasshoppers 100 m (330 ft) away; a human could only see them 30 m (100 ft) away. Some species may see even better – up to eight times as well as people. Raptors also hear very well, especially owls (p. 51) and some harriers. The only bird of prey that uses its nose to find food is the turkey vulture. It's hard to sniff out supper while flying at high speed.

EYE STORY
The eyes of a eurasian buzzard (skull above) can be as big as an adult human's eyes, although the human weighs 50 times as much!

Nictitating membrane protects and cleans the eye

PROTECTIVE EYEBROW
Raptors such as this ferruginous hawk have a very obvious eyebrow called the "supraorbital ridge" (p. 11). The ridge may shade the eye from the sun when hunting, or protect it from injury when hitting prey, or crashing through trees in a chase.

Rather small brain tilts to fit into back of skull

Hole for the ear, normally covered in feathers

EARS AND SPEED
The ear hole is small but important. Sound is used for calling, recognizing mates, and locating prey. Falcons, such as the peregrine (skull on left), rely less on hearing than do owls and some harriers, which fly slow and low, listening for prey.

THE BEAUTIFUL BITE
Falcons, such as this saker falcon, have large heads for their size. All falcons have an extra serration on each side of the beak, called the "toral tooth", which they use, as well as their feet, for killing quarry. Other birds of prey do all their killing with their feet, saving their beaks for eating.

"Toral tooth" to kill prey

Eyes and beak take up a lot of room; brain is not so big

EYE WIPER
The eye of this Verreaux's eagle looks clouded over, but there is nothing wrong. The cloudy surface is in fact a third eyelid called the "nictitating membrane". This membrane is a tough, clear skin that can flick across the eye and keep it clean without stopping the bird from being able to see. It is often closed on impact with prey to protect the eye.

The eagle can see at least twice as far as the man, probably further

THE USES OF THE TONGUE
Raptors, like dogs, pant to lose heat – as this golden eagle is doing. They breathe through a hole halfway along their tongues. And they use their tongues to hook food back from the tips of their beaks so that they can swallow it.

Little is known about raptors' sense of taste; some captive birds show definite likes and dislikes

GREAT EYES, NO BRAINS
It is hard to know exactly how far an eagle can see. There is no doubt, however, that a golden eagle can see a rabbit at least 1.6 km (1 mile) away, and probably more. Its brain is not so impressive. The cleverest birds of prey are the vultures.

Brain area of the bird of prey

Brown snake eagle skull

HEAD TURNER
Birds of prey have such enormous eyes that they cannot move them in the sockets. Instead, they can see all round by turning their heads with their long, flexible necks. They like to look at the world from many angles and will even turn their heads to look at life from upside down.

Young African fish eagles have brown and white heads; adults' heads are pure white

This sub-adult bird's head is gradually turning pure white

Small brain

Eyes face forwards, so that their fields of vision overlap (this is called binocular vision) which enables the bird to judge distance

HUNTERS' EYES FACE FORWARDS
Raptors, such as this black kite, have forward-facing eyes, like other hunting animals (including humans). This gives them the ability to judge depth and distance, which is vital for successful hunting (pp. 50–51).

VOICE OF AFRICA
African fish eagles are very noisy and use their loud calls to welcome their mates. Raptors use their voices in many ways, from chicks begging their parents for food, to the excited calls made during aggressive encounters, to the softer noises of courtship.

White-backed vultures are not really bald; the head and neck are covered in a fine down

Supraorbital ridge

Piercing eye of vulture scans wide areas for carcasses, from high above

NO NEED FOR KNIFE AND FORK
Vultures, such as this white-backed vulture, have very strong necks and beaks to help them tear through the tough skin of large animals. Big vultures, such as the lappet-faced vulture in Africa and the Andean condor, can break through the skin on dead buffaloes and whales! If smaller vultures find such big animals first, they have to wait for larger birds to arrive and rip them open before they can feed. The smaller birds' beaks are not strong enough to cut through such tough skin.

Crest is only half-extended

Thin but powerful beak

Turkey vultures are probably the only raptors to smell out their food

Nares (nostrils) are completely see-through

SENDING SIGNALS
Many birds of prey have a crest. No one really knows why they have them, but it may be so that they can signal their moods to other birds of the same kind. A raised crest probably means the bird is angry. Crests vary in length. The changeable hawk eagle (left) has a short crest.

A NOSE FOR FOOD
The only bird of prey known to have a good sense of smell is the turkey vulture. In the forests of the Americas, it flies very slowly over the tree canopy trying to locate dead animals by smell. Other species of vulture wait for the turkey vulture to find food and then follow it down to eat.

People need aids such as binoculars; human sight is far weaker than that of an eagle

Skeletons

White-tailed sea eagle

IN SOME BIRDS OF PREY, the skeleton weighs less than the feathers. For example, the skeleton of a male European sparrowhawk is only about 11% of its total body-weight. This lightness is necessary if the birds are to fly – the heaviest flying bird in the world weighs only 16 kg (35 lb), and fast-flying, agile birds weigh a fraction of that. Many of the larger bones are hollow and filled with air to make them light. At the same time, the skeleton has to be strong enough to anchor and support the powerful flying muscles, and to protect the internal organs. It needs to be rigid enough to hold the muscles in place, yet flexible enough to withstand heavy stresses.

Wedge-tailed eagles have 14 cervical (neck) vertebrae

The coracoid links the sternum and the shoulder area

Shoulder muscles are attached to the scapula

Lower jaw can only move straight up and down; birds do not chew, they only bite and rip off chunks of flesh

The five thoracic vertebrae, in the centre of the back above the synasacrum, are fused together

Bones of pelvis, lower back vertebrae and most of tail vertebrae are fused in one unit of bone, the synasacrum

Wedge-tailed eagle

The caudal (tail) vertebrae give firm yet flexible support to the muscles of the tail; the last six vertebrae are fused

Sternum

Knee joint

Tibia (lower leg bone) fused with some of upper foot bones in the tibiotarsus

This is the bird's ankle

ANCHORS FOR MUSCLES
The four bones of the pectoral girdle anchor the flight muscles: the shoulder muscles attach to the scapula, the breast muscles to the sternum and furcula (wishbone). The coracoid links shoulders and breast. This girdle is attached flexibly to the rest of the body, so that it can move easily, relative to the rest of the skeleton, as the bird flies.

BONES TO FLY WITH
Bird skeletons follow the same basic pattern as human skeletons, but a number of the bones are fused together to give the rigidity needed to support the flight muscles. The bones of the pelvis are fused to give a strong platform for the leg and tail muscles.

White-tailed sea eagle

Most foot bones are fused together in the tarsometatarsus, which acts as an extension of the leg (pp. 24–25)

Jaws are lightweight struts to support beak

Eyes take up much more space than brain does

Secretary bird skull

LIKE A HONEYCOMB
Although birds' major bones are hollow, they are strong, because they have internal struts across them (above). Such bones are called pneumatic bones, because they are filled with air, and some are attached to the air sacs of the bird's respiratory system (p. 22). If a bird breaks a major wing bone, it can actually breathe through the break.

LOOK, MA, NO TEETH
Birds save weight by having no teeth, and light jawbones. They can do this because "chewing" happens in the gizzard section of the stomach. The thick, muscular walls and sandpaper-like inner surface of the gizzard grind and break down birds' food.

Bones of skull are extensively fused to protect head with minimum of weight

Egyptian vulture skull

Sclerotic ring supports the huge eyeball

Skull is paper-thin, yet very strong

This joint is the bird equivalent of the human wrist; the bones beyond it are the equivalent to the bones of the hand

Tendons from the main flight muscles attach to the humerus, which is short and strong to take the stress

Golden eagle head

BETTER THAN A RUBBER NECK
Humans have seven vertebrae in their necks; birds have from 13 to 25, depending on the species. This long neck enables them to preen and clean virtually their whole bodies. It also gives them the ability to look round directly behind them.

Bird equivalent to human forearm

The bones that would be hand bones in a human are fused together in the last section of the wing

Sparrowhawk skeleton

The two, paired clavicles form the furcula (wishbone)

Bird-hunting raptors have particularly long, slender toes

LIGHTER THAN FEATHERS
In smaller birds the skeleton is very fine, paper-thin in places, yet still able to withstand high speed flight, and high-speed impact as the birds catch their prey. This skeleton weighs less than the sparrowhawk's feathers.

Long, supple neck, which is supported by a complex muscle structure, enabling very precise movement

Neck tucked in to ruff of feathers to keep warm

Vultures

VULTURES ARE THE REFUSE COLLECTORS, or scavengers, of the raptor world. They prevent disease by eating dead animals before they decay. In Africa, they eat far more meat than all other predators put together – an estimated 25 million kg (25,000 tons) each year on the Serengeti plains alone. Vultures, especially big vultures, are good at soaring but bad at flapping flight (pp. 16–19), so most live in hot places or in mountainous areas. There are two separate groups: New World vultures in the Americas and Old World vultures elsewhere. Both groups range from huge birds over 10 kgs (22 lbs) in weight to small species of only 2–3 kg (4–7 lb). The largest, condors, have 3-m (10-ft) wings.

3-m (10-ft) wingspan

CONDORS
The Andean condor (above) soars above the Andes mountains of South America. Some glide right across to the Pacific coast and scavenge dead whales. The Californian condor (p. 59) recently became extinct in the wild, but birds bred in captivity are now being released to re-establish the species.

New World vultures urinate over their legs and feet, perhaps to cool themselves

Juveniles have dark brown plumage, adults have white

Bright yellow face; neck not bare, unlike most vultures'

Wings outstretched to keep its balance

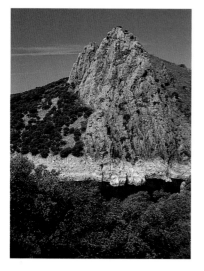

HOME WITH A VIEW
Many vultures breed in the mountains where predators cannot reach them, as at "Vulture Rock" in Spain (above). Some species nest alone in caves, others in large groups called colonies.

OLD WORLD
Old World vultures are related to kites and eagles, whereas New World vultures are related to storks, and only distantly to the other birds of prey. The smallest of the Old World vultures are Egyptian vultures (above). There are two kinds: the Indian race have yellow beaks and the European and African races have black beaks.

NEW WORLD
The turkey vulture is the smallest of the New World vultures, and has the largest range (lives over the widest area). It is found from southern Canada to Argentina. It has a better sense of smell than other birds of prey (pp. 30–31), which it uses to sniff out dead animals in the forests of the Americas.

Turkey vulture gets its name from its red face

Neck feathers can be pulled down like a ruff when the bird is hot or feeding, and pulled up when it is cold

New World vultures have chicken-like feet

The tail sticks up when it is doing its bouncing walk

The dropped head can mean different things, including aggression

DINNER PARTY: NO JACKET REQUIRED
Vultures gather in dozens to eat large carcasses. In Africa up to six different species may gather at once, plus rival scavengers such as marabou storks. Some vultures appear to be there for social reasons, and don't actually eat. A large group of vultures can strip an antelope carcass bare in 30 minutes, and a cow in three hours.

Marabou storks – carrion-eating storks

Eurasian griffon skull

Upper mandible fixed to the skull

Lower mandible moves, much like our jaw

WATCHER IN THE SKY
All vultures have excellent (daylight) eyesight. As they soar, they watch for signs of death, and watch one another. If one bird starts to drop, its neighbours follow, then their neighbours, and so vultures can come in from nearly 300 km (200 miles) away to a carcass. Eurasian griffons such as this belong to the family of Old World vultures called griffon vultures, or just griffons.

COMMON BUT CLEAN
White-backed vultures are the most common in Africa. They have bare heads and necks, like most vultures, because they put their heads inside carcasses. Feathered heads would get very mucky. All vultures love to bathe and, after they have fed, will fly long distances to wash.

Huge wings give vultures their soaring ability

A white-backed vulture can eat 1 kg (2.2 lb) of meat in two minutes

THESE FEET WERE MADE FOR WALKING
Some vultures like to walk, in fact the American black vulture (below) literally bounces along on strong legs. When hunting for small dead animals, like crabs or baby turtles, it spends much of its time on the ground. Black vultures' legs and feet have evolved to make them more sure-footed than other vultures.

Black vultures can run or bounce along at quite a fast rate

Ospreys and fish eagles

OSPREYS ARE UNIQUE. Found in most parts of the world, they are perfectly adapted for catching fish, and eat almost nothing else. To help them to grip their slippery food their talons are extra-curved, and they have scales on the soles of their feet and specially adapted toes (p. 24). They soar high above the water to spot their prey, then dive steeply down to seize it, and they are the only raptors that will go completely underwater to catch a fish. The eight species of fish eagle are not such specialists. They do catch fish, and, like ospreys, have extra-curved talons and scaly soles to their feet. But they also scavenge a lot, and will eat just about anything they can find or catch. Unlike ospreys, fish eagles usually catch fish by still hunting – quietly sitting and waiting for fish to swim by, then diving (at a shallower angle than ospreys) and dipping their feet into the water to scoop up a surface-swimming fish. They include the bald eagle and the huge Steller's sea eagle.

BORN TO FISH
Ospreys have long legs to help them catch fish under the water, and their outer toes can be swung backwards to help them to grip their slippery prey better (p. 25). Their plumage tends to be more waterproof than other raptors'. They can even close up their noses to stop water rushing in.

Osprey's wings sweep back in the final dive into the water

Fish is held with its nose facing the front to reduce drag

ARC OF A DIVER
Ospreys usually take fish close to the water surface. They can, however, plunge into the water, leaving only the tips of their wings showing. They soar, circle, and even hover over water as they look for quarry, then dive in, throwing their feet forward to snatch the fish. After resting a few moments on the water, they pull out with strong, horizontal wing beats.

SYMBOL OF AMERICA
The bald eagle was chosen as the national emblem of the United States in 1782. Benjamin Franklin disapproved of the choice because bald eagles steal food from others. He believed the turkey should become the emblem. The eagle won the day. In recent decades it became endangered, as a result of persecution and pollution. Great efforts were made to save the symbol of the nation, and the species is now much recovered.

Eagle holds olive branch to symbolize peace

Other foot holds arrows to symbolize war

Ospreys have narrow heads, with no bony ridges above their eyes

Sturdy nests withstand storms on exposed coasts

FAMILY HOME
Ospreys use the same nest year after year, and even generation after generation. It can become very big as it is added to each year. All sorts of materials are added to it, even bones, old rope, cardboard, and plastic bags, although these can entangle and kill the growing young. Some ospreys nest in reed-beds, or on the ground on treeless islands.

These eagles have loud and raucous voices

VARIED DIET
The white-bellied sea eagle lives along the coasts of India, southeast Asia, and Australia. As well as fish, it hunts rabbits, fruit bats, gulls, water birds, even poisonous sea snakes. In some places it now suffers from the effects of the lethal pesticide DDT (p. 13).

WAITING FOR THE FEAST

Every year, Pacific salmon swim upriver, lay their eggs, and die. Bald eagles gather to feed (p. 29). It is possible to see 2,000 of them on one river in Alaska in this season. Fish eagles' broad wings enable them to fly carrying prey heavier than they are, if they need to. Bald eagles can carry 3 kg (7 lb) salmon, and one flew away with a 7 kg (15 lb) deer. Steller's sea eagles can probably carry even heavier loads.

The eagles just sit and wait for the salmon to die

Steller's sea eagle is instantly recognizable by its enormous beak

THE EAGLE HAS LANDED, AGAIN

The white-tailed sea eagle is one of the largest species of eagle. It has been hunted and persecuted by humans for centuries. The last white-tailed sea eagle in Britain was shot in 1916 and the species became extinct there. Gradually, people have become more aware of their responsibilities to the environment, and in the 1960s white-tailed sea eagles were released into the wild on a remote Scottish island. The bird is still rare in Britain, but its numbers are growing.

THE BIG-BEAKED BIG BROTHER

Steller's sea eagles are the largest of all the fish-eating birds of prey. They live on the coast of Russia and China and live mainly on Pacific salmon. They will also catch large birds, such as geese, and mammals such as hares, and even young seals. Like all fish eagles, Steller's sea eagles lay two to three eggs and rear more than one young per clutch (unlike some of the true eagles, p. 12).

Supra-orbital ridge

This juvenile bird does not yet have the full adult plumage

Powerful beak can tear through tough fish skin with ease

Sea eagle swallows bones with the flesh

Strong feet with rough scales to hold the slippery catch

Tail slowly turns white as eagle reaches adult breeding age

Salmon are the favourite food of many northern eagles

Kites and harriers

Male drops food to female

KITES ARE VERY GRACEFUL flyers, easily recognized in flight by their forked tails. There are 33 species. The largest, the European red kite, weighs 12 times as much as the smallest, the South American pearl kite, which weighs about 100 g (3.5 oz). Many of the smaller species eat insects, others hunt for larger quarry, some are scavengers, and some even fish. The 13 species of harriers, and three related species, all have huge wingspans and light bodies, which allow them to fly very slowly while looking and listening for potential prey. All tend to live in open areas: marsh, grasslands, or farmed land.

Swallow-tailed kite in flight

AEROBATIC LUNCH
The male harrier does not usually bring food to the nest. Instead, he calls to the female who flies to meet him. He flies over her and drops food, which she catches with her feet and brings back to the nest. He hunts again.

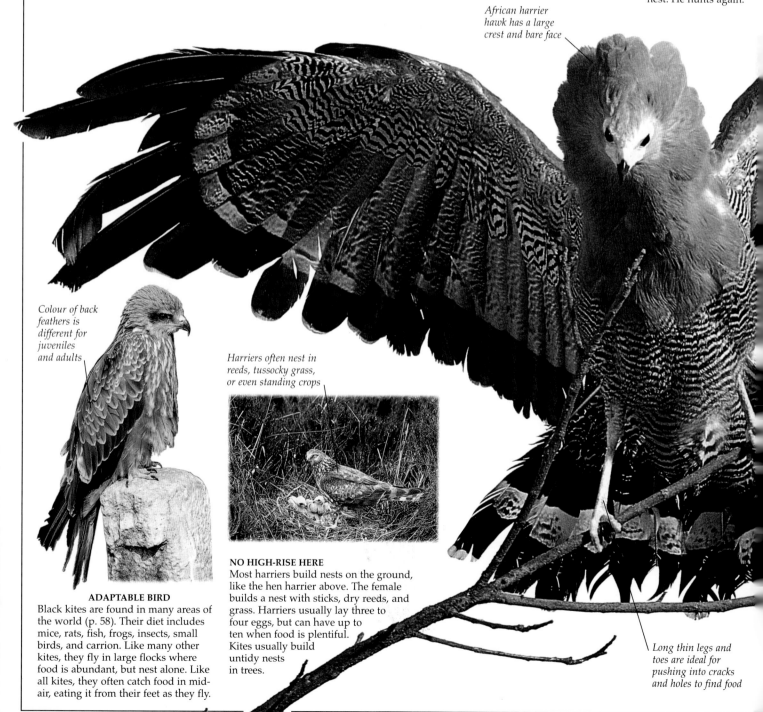

African harrier hawk has a large crest and bare face

Colour of back feathers is different for juveniles and adults

Harriers often nest in reeds, tussocky grass, or even standing crops

NO HIGH-RISE HERE
Most harriers build nests on the ground, like the hen harrier above. The female builds a nest with sticks, dry reeds, and grass. Harriers usually lay three to four eggs, but can have up to ten when food is plentiful. Kites usually build untidy nests in trees.

ADAPTABLE BIRD
Black kites are found in many areas of the world (p. 58). Their diet includes mice, rats, fish, frogs, insects, small birds, and carrion. Like many other kites, they fly in large flocks where food is abundant, but nest alone. Like all kites, they often catch food in mid-air, eating it from their feet as they fly.

Long thin legs and toes are ideal for pushing into cracks and holes to find food

CRADLE SNATCHER
Three species of raptor are closely related to harriers. The African harrier hawk looks very similar, with huge wings and a small body-weight. Its ankle is double-jointed (bends both backwards and forwards) which helps it to get its foot into holes in cliffs and hollow trees, to hook out baby birds to eat. It flies very slowly through trees, looking for likely holes to raid. A similar bird, the crane hawk, found in South American forests, hunts the same way.

PART OF THE FAMILY
Yellow-billed kites are the African sub-species of the black kite. They are a slightly different colour and have a yellow bill (beak).

Kites can twist and turn in an amazing fashion

Most kites have a forked tail; in some species much more forked than this

Red kite has a pale iris

Harriers sometimes fly at a height of less than 1 m (3 ft) as they hunt

SUCCESS STORY
In developed countries, a number of raptors suffered huge declines in recent decades, due largely to pesticides and other features of modern farming. A number of these species have recovered greatly. The red kite was once the commonest kite in Britain, then was reduced to a small, declining population in Wales. It has now been reintroduced into England and Scotland, and is thriving.

SLOWLY DOES IT
Harriers hunt by flying low and slow over marsh, moor, and grasslands, methodically zig-zagging to cover all the ground over which they are hunting. They listen for sounds in the grass – some even have a facial disc to sharpen their sight and hearing, like owls. They eat prey up to the size of a small rabbit.

Large flocks of kites will scavenge for food on rubbish dumps

Reddish colour of feathers gives this species its name

NOT FUSSY, NOR FEARFUL
Kites are not afraid of humans – in Africa, some have learnt to snatch sandwiches from people's hands when they eat outside. Kites will go into towns and rubbish dumps to find scraps to eat. However, they run the risk of picking up poisonous food, or getting bits of plastic or string caught around them.

Long tail aids slow flying

Kites are easy to identify in flight by their forked tails

Hawks and buzzards

North American Swainson's hawks, like other hawks, often hunt from man-made perches such as telegraph poles

HAWKS ARE MOSTLY forest birds. They are fast-flying and very agile, with short, rounded wings which help them twist and turn quickly through trees as they chase after quarry. They also have very long tails which help in steering and act as brakes, enabling them to stop quickly. Buzzards are very adaptable birds. They live and hunt in a wide range of environments, especially part-wooded and cultivated land. They are less agile than hawks, with longer, broader wings and shorter tails. They scavenge where they can and take a variety of prey. Unlike hawks, they soar a lot, watching out for food from high in the sky.

LOOK AT THOSE LEGS
There are about 20 species of buzzard around the world, including the long-legged buzzard (left). All buzzards are stocky, with thick legs and powerful feet because they mainly catch mammals (p. 25). For most buzzards, rabbits and rodents are the main prey.

Harris' hawks tend to fly more slowly (and use their brains more) than true hawks

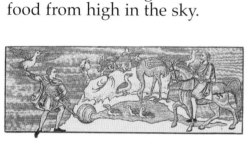

BEST OF HUNTERS
In medieval Europe, the goshawk was known as the "cook's bird", not because it was flown by cooks but because it caught so much food with which to fill the larder. Sparrowhawks were less popular because they catch smaller prey, but were still flown. Buzzards were probably used to train apprentice falconers, as buzzards are slower than hawks, and easier to train.

Sparrowhawk plucks feathers from blackbird before eating it

DON'T EAT THE FEATHERS
Like many other raptors, hawks pluck the feathers from their prey before eating. They often have "plucking posts" near their nests, where they take prey to pluck it. Hawks are divided into the (larger) goshawks and the (smaller) sparrowhawks. There are about 20 species of goshawk, and about 25 species of sparrowhawk. Goshawks hunt both "fur and feather" – both mammals and birds; sparrowhawks usually catch small birds. Hawks often hunt by flitting from perch to perch, skimming the ground between trees so that prey will not spot them.

Hawk-like tail and wings give great agility

Hawks can take relatively big prey: female sparrowhawks catch wood pigeons which are heavier than they are, as well as blackbirds such as this

Hawks often use hedges and trees as cover as they fly towards prey, only "breaking cover" and showing themselves at the last moment

FEEDING THE KIDS
Numbers of Eurasian buzzard (above) rise and fall with prey populations. In Britain, the number of breeding buzzards crashed when the disease myxomatosis killed off most rabbits, then rose tenfold in 12 years as rabbit numbers recovered.

HAWK OR BUZZARD?
The Harris' hawk is an unusual bird because it falls between the hawk and buzzard families. Its scientific name is parabuteo which means "like a buzzard". It has the characteristic hawk shape, with long tail and short, rounded wings. It resembles buzzards in its relaxed temperament (hawks tend to be highly-strung). It is unusually sociable. It hunts in groups (p. 27) and breeds co-operatively: parents are helped in rearing chicks by other Harrises in the group.

Alula, or "false wing", helps with stopping and low-speed flight (p. 17)

Harris' hawks are also called bay-winged hawks because of the brown colour on the top of their wings

The larger hawks have strong legs; the smaller sparrowhawks, which prey on birds not mammals, have thinner, less strong legs with very long toes

Eagles

AROUND THE WORLD the eagle is seen as the king of the birds. Many kings, nations, armies, and empires have taken eagles as their symbols. There are over 40 species of eagle, and several distinct groups. The forest eagles include the crowned eagles of Africa, Philippine eagles (p. 56), and South American harpy eagles (p. 59), which are probably the most powerful of all raptors. The true eagles live in open country. Some, such as golden eagles, wedge-tailed eagles, and martial eagles, can have wingspans of over 2.5 m (8 ft). Forest eagles have shorter, more rounded wings and longer tails than true eagles. Snake eagles have thick scales on their legs and feet, instead of feathers, to protect them from snake bites, and short, strong toes to grasp the snakes with.

CHILD SNATCHER?
Many eagles eat carrion, and have been seen feeding on prey much bigger than anything they could kill. This has led to myths developing about eagles carrying off calves, sheep, and even human babies. For all the stories of eagles carrying off children, there is no verified record of an eagle killing a child.

JUNGLE EAGLE
Most forest eagles belong to the family of hawk eagles. The African hawk eagle (right) is one. Hawk eagles, and the other forest eagles, are a similar shape to hawks. Like hawks, they can turn very fast and so can hunt successfully amid thick trees. Sadly, a number of forest eagles are becoming rare as the forests that they live in are steadily cut down.

Striped breast feathers act as camouflage when eagle sits in trees

COMMON PIRATE
Tawny eagles are among the most numerous of eagles. Like many other eagles, they mainly scavenge, eating from carcasses, and even human rubbish. They often act as "pirates", chasing other raptors that have just caught prey, and stealing it.

All true eagles have feathers down to their toes, as do some forest eagles

Eagles which have feathers down to their toes are sometimes called "booted eagles"

IMPERIAL SYMBOL
Eagles have been the symbols of many great empires, including ancient Rome, the Russia of the tsars, and the Austrian Habsburg empire. Roman legions used to carry eagle standards as their symbols and rallying-points (above). To lose the legion's eagle was the worst of all possible disasters.

Birds often pick a dead branch high up as a look-out point

Eagle spreads wings to make it look larger and more threatening

Warthog is defending its baby from the eagle

BABY WARTHOG SNATCHER
The giant martial eagle is the biggest of all the African eagles and one of the largest eagles in the world. Martial eagles have huge feet, and are powerful enough to kill jackals and small antelopes, let alone baby warthogs. They live in open country, on the plains of Africa, and rarely still hunt, preferring to stoop down from the air to catch their prey. In this picture, the eagle is threatening a baby warthog, which is being defended by an adult warthog.

Nictitating membrane protects and cleans eye

FAMILY HOME
Golden eagles return to the same nest sites year after year to raise their young (right). Good nesting sites stay in use: when one pair stops breeding, another uses the nest. Golden eagles come into adult plumage when they are about five. The adult plumage shows that they are fully mature and ready to breed.

Chicks cheep to stimulate their mother to feed them

Brown plumage of young bateleur changes gradually into adult plumage

Golden eagle gets its name from the (relatively) gold-coloured feathers on the back of its head and neck

ACROBAT OF THE AIR
A dull brown juvenile bateleur eagle (above) grows into a brightly-coloured adult (left), reaching maturity at seven. Bateleurs are closely related to the snake eagle family, but eat mainly carrion. They were given the name "bateleur", which means balancer or tightrope walker, because they are so acrobatic in the air.

Fork half-way along tongue helps bird to pull food back into its throat

RELIGIOUS RAPTOR
The eagle is a religious symbol in many cultures, from Native American to Indian. In some religions, an eagle represents the sun, or a god – often a sky god. In Christianity the eagle came to be a symbol of John the evangelist (above), one of the first disciples of Jesus Christ.

Some golden eagles have wingspans of more than 2.5 m (8 ft)

Contour feathers (p. 21) give shape to wing

Golden eagles help farmers by killing rabbits, which compete with sheep for grass

Stocky build is characteristic of golden eagles

MODERATE EATER
Golden eagles live in the tundra areas of the northern hemisphere. Like most eagles, they kill prey much smaller than they are, although they may feed off large dead animals. The biggest exception is Africa's crowned eagle. Crowned eagles have been known to kill antelopes weighing up to 20 kg (45 lb).

This 2 kg (4.5 lb) rabbit will last the 4 kg (9 lb) eagle for two days

The secretary bird

SECRETARY BIRDS have been described as "long-legged marching eagles". Their long legs make them look almost like storks, but they have the hooked raptor beak and, like all birds of prey, they kill with their feet. They live in Africa south of the Sahara, in almost every region which can offer them grasslands, desert edges, or farmed land in which to live. They also need a flat-topped tree to nest in. About 1.2 m (4 ft) high, they weigh 2–4 kg (4.5–9 lb), and have a wingspan of 2 m (6.5 ft) or more. They cannot live in forests because it is too tricky for them to take off and fly amid the trees, and they avoid very thick, tall grass. They flush prey out by walking, not flying, through the long African grass, and then they kill it by stamping on it, with great force and accuracy. Famous for killing snakes, they also eat a wide variety of insects, small animals, and birds.

THE REASON FOR THE NAME
One story is that the long feathers on secretary birds' heads were reminiscent of European secretaries with quill pens behind their ears (above). Or the name may come from the Arabic saqr-tair – "hunting bird".

Two-week-old secretary bird

The same bird at six weeks old

THE YOUNG SECRETARY BIRD
When first hatched, young secretary birds have huge heads. Their legs grow so fast that the scales can't keep up, and in the first few days the old scales split off and new scales grow again and again. They cannot stand up until almost full-grown, which means that they cannot fall out of the nest until ready to fly, or at least glide. Secretary birds are mostly thriving in the wild. They are valuable to farmers because they kill snakes and rodents, although some people still hunt them.

Primary feathers are black; secretary birds can fly and soar very well when they want to

Long quill-like crest feathers

Eyelashes are longer and more beautiful than any human's

Facial skin goes bright orange as bird matures

The two centre tail feathers are twice as long as all the rest

Scales protect the long, powerful legs against snake bites

Back toe used when striking snakes' heads

SLIDES DOWN NICELY

Secretary birds eat snakes the way they eat most of their prey: they swallow them whole. Snakes take longer to go down than their other quarry, slowly being sucked in. Secretary birds have a unique method of killing prey but, as with all raptors, it involves their feet. They stamp on their quarry, repeatedly if necessary. When killing insects they hit with any part of the foot, but when tackling snakes they strike with the back talon at the head of the snake, which is its most vulnerable yet also most dangerous part.

Crest raised, quill feathers up

Crest not raised, quill feathers down

DOMESTIC BLISS

Secretary birds will not even attempt to breed unless the food supply is plentiful. They lay two to three eggs, but usually only one chick survives. In some pairs, both parents take turns to incubate the eggs, whereas in most raptors the female does all the incubating. When sitting on the nest, they often crouch very low to be invisible from the ground.

HIGH-RISE FLAT

Because secretary birds are big and clumsy, they build their nests on top of flat-topped trees. Flat-topped acacia trees are the favourite. First the birds trample the top until it is completely squashed, and then they add sticks and twigs to make a platform, which can be up to 2.5 m (8 ft) across. Tufts of grass and reeds are carried up to make a soft lining for the eggs to lie in, and the chicks to grow in. Some nests are used year after year until they collapse, or are stolen by other raptors.

BUFFET LUNCH

Snakes are only a small part of a secretary bird's diet. The bulk of their food consists of insects such as grasshoppers, locusts, and large beetles. They also catch lizards, hedgehogs, mongooses, birds, rats, mice, and other mammals up to the size of a small hare. Also on the menu are eggs and baby birds. All but the largest items are swallowed whole.

Locust

Lizard

Egg

Mouse

Chick

TILL DEATH DO US PART

Once secretary birds have found a mate, they usually stay together for life. Unlike most raptors, they stay living in their nest together all year, not just when breeding. The paired birds tend to stay within sight of each other during the day, hunting, walking, and flying together, unless the female is brooding eggs or young. Then they sleep lying down together at night. Other raptors that mate for life include bald eagles, golden eagles, African fish eagles, ospreys, and peregrine falcons.

Grass snake disappearing down secretary bird's throat; a good supper

The falcon family

Game bird being struck in mid-air

Falcon stoops past after strike, but will turn to grab the prey

THE BIG FALCONS – sakers, lanners, peregrines, and gyrfalcons – are probably the fastest-flying of all the birds of prey and, when they stoop (dive), the fastest birds in the world (p. 58). They live in open country, such as desert edges, tundra, moor, and grasslands. There are also various smaller true falcons, including kestrels. Forest falcons are small, little-known birds which live in tropical rainforests. The smallest members of the falcon family, and the smallest raptors of all (p. 58), are pygmy falcons. Caracaras don't look or behave much like falcons, but they belong to the same family (p. 11). They come from Latin America and spend much of their time on the ground, scratching under logs and stones searching for food.

The hobby is a small falcon, so agile it can catch swifts in mid-air

CATCHING PREY
Many falcons catch their prey by flying high above it, stooping down at high speed behind it, and then striking it in mid-air. Sometimes a falcon will grasp the prey in the air. This is called "binding to it". However, often the falcon will hit the prey as it dives past, and then either pick up the dead bird on the ground or catch it in mid-air before it hits the ground.

Caracaras have a different wing-shape from that of falcons

THE ODD RELATIVES
Caracaras may not behave much like falcons, but scientists tell us that they are closely related. Rather than hunting in the air, they scavenge like vultures. They are clever birds, and will often annoy campers in the Andes by stealing food from their camps.

BARS OF YOUTH
A falcon's juvenile plumage has downward bars on the chest, and the shoulders and back feathers have buff edging. This plumage usually goes in the first moult, but it allows the bird to hunt in adult territory before it grows adult plumage (p. 15). Falcons born in hot countries often look much paler than those hatching in cooler ones, because the sun bleaches out the colour in the feathers.

Heavily striped breast of immature lanner

Juvenile male lanner

Notch, or tooth, on falcon's beak

Adult male lanner

Spots of adult plumage

FLYING HUNTER
Lanners live in some parts of Europe and the Middle East, and all over Africa except for the rainforest and the Sahara. They catch small birds in the air, and also insects, small mammals, and reptiles. They are numerous in Africa but rare in Europe. A programme in Israel to breed them and release them into the wild is doing well.

Short tail means falcons can't manoeuvre as well as hawks

Side-view of juvenile to show back feathers

Side-view of adult to show back feathers

Peregrine falcon nesting on a cliff ledge

CHOOSING A HOME
Like owls, falcons don't build nests. Smaller falcons and forest falcons use disused nests or holes in trees. Larger falcons tend to use ledges on cliffs, rocks, or buildings. They dig scrapes in the soil and dirt on the ledge, then lay their eggs.

Young members of the rarest species of falcon in the world, the Mauritius kestrel

Kestrels are a common sight in many towns

BIRD ABOUT TOWN
Kestrels, and some other falcons, have learnt that high-rise buildings are a little like cliffs, with ledges and alcoves which make good nesting places. They have also learnt that where humans live, so do many other animals which the falcon can use as a food source. There are problems though – young birds may get run over before they learn to deal with traffic.

TAKING TIME TO LOOK AROUND
The 13 species of kestrel round the world are all able to hover (p. 19), some better than others. This enables them to "perch" in mid-air, giving them time to spot small animals on the ground, which other falcons are moving too fast to see. So they are able to catch more small mammals than the other falcons, which eat mostly birds.

NOWHERE TO RUN TO
Mauritius kestrels almost became extinct recently, mainly because of the destruction of the forests on their home island. A breeding and release scheme has saved them, for the time being. Small populations of any raptor are always vulnerable, especially if they live on islands (p. 59).

Contour feathers have buff edges in immature plumage

Sub-adult female lanner

Juvenile stripes are lost in the first moult, after which the bird is sub-adult (p. 15)

Falcons' toes are even longer than hawks' toes

UNISEX FEATHERS?
In some raptors, males and females have different colour plumage. Usually the difference doesn't show until the birds have their adult plumage. American kestrels are one exception: the difference is obvious as soon as they have feathers. This sub-adult female lanner (left) is pretty much the same colour as a sub-adult male. The only real difference is that the female is usually about a third heavier than the male. This is about average for falcons (p. 9).

This dark bar is called the moustachial strip

Adult female lanner

Crop area is often less marked than the lower breast

INDIVIDUAL MARKINGS
You can tell a lot about a bird from its feathers. Within each species, there is a certain amount of variation in plumage. Individuals differ and so, in many species, do birds from different regions. Some lanners are more heavily marked than others and some have a redder colour to the back of the head. Adult lanners from southern Africa have a pink breast with no markings; northern lanners tend to be very heavily marked.

Tail feathers are used in steering, and as brakes

47

Owls

When the night comes, owls take over from the other raptors. They hunt by stealth, flying slowly, softly, silently to surprise their prey. They rely on their ears more than their eyes to find their quarry. Most, though not all, are nocturnal (night hunters), or hunt at dawn and dusk. They range in size from the tiny elf owl, which weighs only 40 g (1.4 oz), up to the European eagle owl, which is a huge 3 kg (6.5 lb). Most owls rest during the day. Their feathers are dull, not bright, to camouflage them from possible predators in the day, and from possible prey at night. The different groups of owls, between them, fill almost all the hunting roles of the diurnal (day-hunting) birds of prey, except for scavenging (carrion is hard to see at night) and the fast flying and diving of the falcons.

Baby owls are soon able to swallow their food, such as this mouse, whole

MIDNIGHT CALLER
The tawny owl has the most famous of owl calls – "too-witt-too-woo". It also makes a shrill "kee-wick" noise late at night. Like many other raptors it likes to catch its prey by still hunting (pp. 26–27): it sits very still and quiet, listening and looking out for movement, then it pounces. It is also known as the brown owl.

SILENT EAGLE OF THE NIGHT
Owls fly on large, silent wings. Their feathers have a fine down all over them, and the leading edges of the outer flight feathers are serrated like a comb. This gives a soft, frayed edge which deadens the noise of their wingbeats so their prey doesn't hear them coming. They are not particularly fast or agile fliers, so they rely on surprise as they float through the night. The largest of all owls are the various eagle owls.

Bengal eagle owl

All feathers are covered in a fine down to aid silent flight

Mottled breast feathers aid camouflage and keep the bird warm in cold weather

Eagle owls have feathered toes, which help to protect their feet from bites

HOOTING BOOBOOK
The boobook owl gets its name from the hooting noise it makes. Several other kinds of owl are named after the sounds they make. For example, there is a barking owl, and even an owl called a saw-whet owl which is said to make a noise like a saw being sharpened. Owls call to attract mates or mark out their territory.

Boobook owl's colouring helps it to be camouflaged during the daytime

Baby owls are covered in a fluffy down to stop them getting cold

Barn owls help farmers by killing mice and rats

BABY OWLS
Baby owls, such as these eagle owls, can often be of very different sizes in the same brood. The mother bird starts sitting on the eggs almost as soon as she has laid the first one, so there can be a large gap between the oldest baby and the youngest. This is called "asynchronous hatching". Owls grow a little more slowly than other birds of prey of similar size.

FARMER'S FRIEND
Barn owls are a little different from other owls: they have a more pronounced facial disk (p. 51), and so even better sight and hearing, and are particularly nocturnal. There are about 12 species, found around the world. They often live on farms because there are lots of mice and rats to hunt. They are known for living in barns, but anywhere secure, weatherproof, and quiet will do – on top of bales of hay, in hollow trees, even on the ground.

Snowy owl's white feathers camouflage it in snow

DAYTIME OWL
Most owls prefer to hunt at night, or at dawn and dusk, but many also have to hunt in the day when raising chicks. The snowy owl and other owls that live in the Arctic have no choice about daylight flying: in the summer the days are so long, there is no night.

Owl's huge eye is vulnerable to damage

Secondary feathers

Primary feathers

ON THE DEFENSIVE
Owls, such as this long-eared owl, can be very fierce when defending themselves or their nests. To make themselves look very fierce they spread their wings and turn them round so the back faces the front (left). This makes them look much bigger than they really are. The pearl spotted owlet has two white patches on the feathers at the back of its head. The patches look like eyes and stare out at any potential hunter.

For many owls, a vole such as this is a favourite food

DOWN IN ONE
Owls, more than other raptors, like to swallow their prey whole if it is small enough. Most owls eat rodents, especially rats, mice, and voles. Many owls, especially small ones, live on insects. Fishing owls eat fish, spectacled owls eat crabs, eagle owls catch rabbits, hares, and even day-flying raptors as they rest at night.

The life of owls

Owls do not build their own nests. Some use holes in trees, others use abandoned buildings, or barns, or even bridges, or take over abandoned nests. One species, the ferocious great horned owl, sometimes even takes over inhabited hawks' nests, killing the occupants. Owls tend to be fairly secretive birds. They hide during the day because all other birds fear them, knowing that owls may kill them at night as they sleep. Even tiny birds like bluetits harass them, and try to drive them away whenever they are seen. Crows and magpies will kill owls if they can.

SITTING PRETTY
Owls, such as this scops owl, perch differently from other raptors (pp. 24–25). Some owls have very strong feet: eagle owls can kill hares, and the feet of one Australian owl earned it the name the powerful owl.

WISE AS AN OWL
Owls have been thought of as being very wise since the time of Ancient Greece. The owl was associated with Athena, the Greek goddess of wisdom. In some parts of the world, owls are birds of ill omen because of their link with the night.

Owl pellets

Contents of pellets

BRINGING UP DINNER
Like many other birds, owls cough up pellets after they have eaten (see pp. 22–23). They swallow indigestible parts of their quarry, such as fur, bones, feathers, and even small shells. Their stomachs make these parts into a bundle and cough it up before the birds feed again.

THE EYES OF A HUNTER
Owls have huge eyes at the front of their heads, as do other hunters, such as lions and humans. Because their eyes are close together hunting animals have binocular vision (p. 31). This means that they can judge depth and distance very well – vital when hunting. Their field of vision is, however, limited. Vegetarian animals, in contrast, which do not need to hunt, usually have eyes on the sides of their heads, so that they can see predators coming from any direction.

They can make a noise like a rattlesnake to scare predators away from their holes

GOING UNDERGROUND
Most owls are solitary, but burrowing owls live in colonies. They nest in old ground squirrel and prairie dog mounds in North America. These tunnels may be as deep as 2.7 m (9 ft) underground. Burrowing owls have less of a facial disc than most owls, because they are mainly diurnal (active in the day), so have less need for extra-fine hearing and sight than nocturnal owls.

Eagle owl skull

Scleral ring, a bony ring which protects most of the eye

Burrowing owls often stand on the top of their mounds to keep a look out for danger

Owl can fit into burrows only 10 cm (4 in) wide

The burrowing owl probably has longer legs for its body size than any other owl

Owls' senses

Owls are famous for their ability to see in the dark. They cannot see in total darkness, but need only the tiniest bit of light. Their hearing is even better: in tests, barn owls have caught mice in total darkness by hearing alone. Most birds have small ear openings; owls have long vertical slits which can be almost as long as the owl's head (p. 15). In some owls, one of the ears is much higher on the bird's head than the other. This makes it easier for the owl to work out where a sound is coming from, and so to hunt down the animal that made it.

Starting facing backwards, an owl can turn its head over 360°

If they start facing forwards, owls can turn their heads 270° each way

Another way to look at life

Owls, such as this juvenile barn owl, can turn their heads in every direction

WHAT A DISH
One of the things that helps owls such as this Bengal eagle owl to see and hear so well is the shape of their faces. They have a facial disk, or dish, which funnels all available light and sound into their eyes and ears, a little bit like a satellite dish. This facial disk is usually marked by a ring of small bristle-type feathers.

Ear tufts are nothing to do with ears; they are probably used to signal moods, such as anger, excitement, and fear

Facial disc gathers light and sound into eyes and ears

Tawny owl with head turned

Mouth is much larger than size of beak would suggest

Birds of prey in history

BIRDS OF PREY have always seemed magical and fascinating to human beings. They are important symbols in ancient cultures all over the world, and in many religions. The eagle, always seen as the king of the birds, represents authority, strength, victory, and pride, and is linked with the sun, royalty, and gods, especially sky gods. The owl may symbolize wisdom, or, because it is a bird of the night, may be linked with death and ill fortune, its cry an evil omen. More practically, people have hunted with raptors since ancient times. As far as is known, falconry was first practised in Central Asia about 4,000 years ago. It has been popular for many centuries in China, India, the Middle East, and Europe.

INDIAN FALCONER
This 17th-century falconer was part of a very ancient tradition. Falconry has long been practised in the Indian sub-continent. The earliest surviving reference to it is from the 2nd century AD, but it may have been practised much earlier. In China, falcons were being used for hunting by the 7th century BC.

Coffin for falcon mummy; the designs are just like those on human mummy cases

MUMMIFIED FALCON
Many ancient Egyptian gods and goddesses were linked with animals and birds, such as the cow, the vulture, and the falcon. Some were even kept in temples to represent these deities. There was a falcon-headed god called Horus, meaning "the lofty one". Falcons such as the one above were mummified and buried in tombs with kings.

Falconers' gloves have traditionally been made of strong leather to stop talons puncturing the hand beneath

Eagle feathers

Training horses to stand having raptors this close is not easy

William brought several species of raptor with him that had not been seen in England before

EARLY BIRDS
This picture comes from the Bayeux tapestry, woven to celebrate William the Conqueror's conquest of England in 1066. The first English falconer was probably an 8th-century Saxon king of Kent, Ethelbert II. The most famous early European falconer was the German emperor Frederick II, who once lost an important battle so that he could go hawking.

*Painted plaster mask
for a falcon mummy*

*The Cooper's hawk
is almost vertical as
it comes in to land*

*This was worn on a
lip plug, which was
inserted through a hole
made in the bottom lip*

FACIAL CHARM
Because raptors have always
been seen as special and precious,
jewellery and statues have often
been made in their image. Eagle
heads like this one were made as
lip ornaments by the Mixtecs of
Mexico, who made most of the
gold work for the famous Aztec
empire. Birds of prey have also
often featured in objects made
for ritual religious use.

*The actual
falcon mummy*

*Hunting straps, a
modern invention*

HAWK MAGIC
To have a wild bird
such as this Cooper's
hawk choose to fly
towards you and land
on your fist is a magical
experience. There is a bond
between falconer and bird. This
has given falconry an appeal to
people in many different cultures,
throughout history. Today, although
falconry is no longer needed to provide
food, its appeal is as strong as ever.

*The Cooper's hawk throws
its legs up high to cushion
the impact of landing*

EAGLES AND THE SPIRIT
The bald eagle and golden
eagle have long been objects
of worship to North American
Indians. Eagles are still
important in the ceremonies
of many Native American
peoples. Their feathers have
often been collected and used
in many decorative ways,
most famously on head-
dresses. This eagle feather
wand (left) was waved to
the music of drums and
rattles in the eagle dance
of the Cherokee tribe.

DESERT SPORT
Falconry has been popular
in the Arab world for
centuries. Originally,
as elsewhere, it was
a means of catching
food, such as bustards
and desert hares. Now it is a sport.
The falcons are often transported to
the hunting grounds in aeroplanes, and
the chase is more likely to be followed
in Land-Rovers than on camels.

Training a bird of prey

ONCE, BIRDS WERE TRAINED to catch prey for humans to eat, but today falconry is a popular sport. It is practised in many parts of the world, including the United States, Europe, the Arab world, and Central Asia. The birds flown range from great eagles to tiny sparrowhawks. The first step in training a bird is to let it know that the trainer is not an enemy, but a friendly source of food. Once this is accomplished, the bird is asked to jump or hop on to the trainer's gloved fist for food. The distance is then increased until the bird is flying 100 m (330 ft) or so to the trainer's fist. Throughout these exercises, the bird is attached to the falconer by a long, fine string. When the bird responds well to the falconer's calls, it can be flown free and the falconer and bird can begin to hunt together.

16th-century English falconer putting a hood on a falcon

Receiver and aerial used by falconer

RADIO CONTROL?
Even birds of prey get lost sometimes, so falconers tie bells to their birds to help locate them. Nowadays, they can use radio tracking equipment called "telemetry". A very small transmitter (left) is attached to the bird before it starts flying. This transmitter sends out a bleep, that can be heard by a special receiver (above), up to a distance of 25 km (15 miles) in perfect weather conditions, most often about 6 km (4 miles). The signal can sometimes be blocked by hills or woods.

Transmitter and bells are clipped to bird

Larger part of jesses removable for safe flying

Smaller part of jesses attached to bird's legs

The hood "hoodwinks" or fools the bird into thinking that it is night, and so time to be calm and still

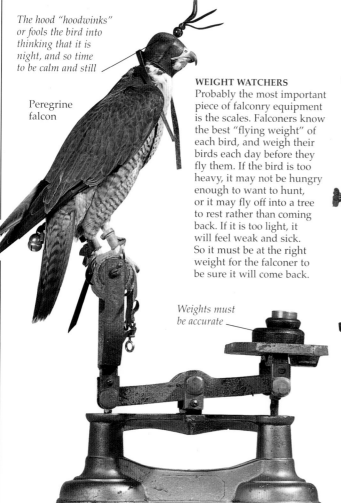
Peregrine falcon

Anglo-Indian hood

Dutch hood

Blocked hood

Arab-style hood

Weights must be accurate

WEIGHT WATCHERS
Probably the most important piece of falconry equipment is the scales. Falconers know the best "flying weight" of each bird, and weigh their birds each day before they fly them. If the bird is too heavy, it may not be hungry enough to want to hunt, or it may fly off into a tree to rest rather than coming back. If it is too light, it will feel weak and sick. So it must be at the right weight for the falconer to be sure it will come back.

Hawk master swivel

Old brass swivel

Hawk and falcon swivel

Sparrowhawk swivel

FURNITURE FOR BIRDS
The trained bird has to wear various pieces of equipment, known as "furniture", so that its handler can control it. It wears leather straps, called jesses, on its legs, so that the falconer can hang onto it – a little like the collar on a dog. The falconer holds long straps attached to the jesses. The straps are threaded through a metal swivel so that they don't become tangled if the bird twists around. If the bird is on an outside perch, it is tethered by a leash threaded through the ring on the swivel.

The falconer's knot has to be tied one-handed as the other hand is carrying the bird

Falconer's bag, with pockets for meat and equipment

Spare pair of jesses kept on bag

Dummy rabbit made for hawks or buzzards to chase

Rabbit lure

Plume on hood acts as handle when putting hood on or taking it off

Falconer's glove

Leash should be wrapped neatly, otherwise it might tangle the bird if the bird jumps or twists around

Old pair of wings with meat attached, used in training

PORTRAIT OF A FALCONER
It takes a long time to learn how to be a falconer. A mistake can cause the loss or even the death of a bird. The bird needs to be flown every day while it is being trained except when it is having a rest to moult. An experienced falconer can have a falcon or buzzard flying free in a two or three weeks, and an eagle in six weeks, although the bird will still have much more to learn.

Belt keeps falconry bag in place

Right-handers hold birds on left hand, left-handers the other way around

Creanse (training line)

Rabbit leg

Larger bits of meat are used to get the birds' attention, smaller bits are given as rewards

Knife

Clippers

Bits of beef

Lure

Items falconers carry in their bags

Around the world

MANY OF THE RAPTORS which breed in the northern hemisphere fly south for the winter (migrate). In 28 species, all the birds migrate each year. In another 42 species, the northernmost birds go south for winter. By flying south in autumn, they avoid cold weather, short days, and less food. By going north in the spring, they can take advantage of longer days in which to hunt, and the abundant food supplies of the northern summer. Migrating can be dangerous: birds have to deal with bad weather and, much worse, people who shoot them. Hundreds of thousands of birds of prey are killed each year along migration routes; not for food, just for fun. Hunting, however, is not the worst of all the problems that raptors face. The greatest threats are habitat destruction and pollution. As the forests of the world are cut down, many raptors lose their homes, and die.

EAGLE IN DANGER
The Philippine eagle is the rarest eagle in the world. The forests that it lives in are disappearing fast. A captive breeding programme is trying to restore its numbers, but it is a very large eagle and needs large areas of undisturbed forest in which to hunt. Unless the forest is saved, this eagle will die out in the wild.

The Philippine eagle is one of the world's largest eagles, with a particularly massive beak

Arrows show direction of major autumn migrations; some raptors migrate much shorter distances

Migrating birds cross mountain ranges by the lowest passes; they are easy to shoot as they fly low over them

Map showing the major raptor migration routes: named places are major concentration points at which very many raptors may be seen

Migration happens over broad fronts, not narrow channels, except at concentration points; the arrows can only indicate the general direction of the most popular migration routes

One unusual migrant, the eastern red-footed, or Amur, falcon begins its migration in this region, and ends it in East Africa, having flown across the Indian Ocean

Falsterbo

Istanbul

Tarifa

Malta

Eilat

Bab al Mandab

Every year five million birds are shot on Malta, including over 100,000 raptors

The second greatest raptor concentration point in the world; over a million raptors pass through each year

Raptors take the routes that involve the shortest sea crossings, gathering at places such as Tarifa, Malta, Istanbul, and Bab al Mandab

The steppe eagle travels all the way from the Russian steppes to South Africa to avoid the winter and eat termites

MIGRATION PATTERNS
Most raptors avoid flying over large areas of water, if possible, because it is too tiring for them. The rising air currents on which they rely to save energy when travelling do not usually form over water (p. 18). Most migrating raptors fly around seas, rather than over them, and hop from island to island if they have to cross the sea. Falcons and harriers rely less on soaring and can sustain flapping flight more easily, so they can fly long distances over water.

Some birds move through the islands of southeast Asia to winter in Australia

SENSELESS SHOOTING
Raptors have been shot ever since people invented guns. The worst slaughter occurs at concentration points on migration routes. These occur where a route is channelled into a narrow stream by water or mountain barriers, or along coastlines and ridges, which birds follow because they give a steady supply of updrafts.

Two dead eagles

Goshawks which live in the far north move south in harsh winters when prey becomes scarce

In flight, air pressure bends primary feathers upwards

The steppe eagle migrates 13,000 km (8,000 miles) each autumn

MARATHON MIGRANTS
Steppe eagles travel from central Russia to South Africa each autumn. Another long-distance migrant is the eastern red-footed, or Amur, falcon. It travels from northern China to East Africa. Unusually, it flies over, not around, the Indian Ocean.

SHOULD I STAY OR SHOULD I GO?
In some species, the birds will only move south in especially cold winters, or only move within their breeding range and not to an entirely different area, or only some of the birds in a region move. This is called "partial migration". A number of species, such as goshawks (above), sparrowhawks, and buzzards, are partial migrants. Often, adult birds can stay farther north than juveniles, because they are better at finding food.

FROM SLAUGHTER TO SANCTUARY
Hawk Mountain in Pennsylvania, in the United States, is on the Kittatinny ridge, along which many raptors migrate. Once, many birds were shot as they flew over Hawk Mountain, but in 1934 it was bought by conservationists, who made it the world's first bird of prey sanctuary. They organized the world's first annual hawk count – since copied around the world – and led research into raptors.

American migrations tend to follow the lines of coasts and ridges, both of which provide plentiful updrafts to save raptors' energy

Cape May

The best place in the world to see raptors; over 2.5 million may pass through in one migration season

Panama Canal

The place and date of the ringing are written on the ring, so that the next scientists to trap the bird can trace its movements

The birds using this route tend to follow the warmer coastline, rather than the colder mountains

Only a few raptors migrate this far south

A RING TO TRACK A RAPTOR WITH
It is hard to know when and where birds travel, and how far. One method scientists use to find out this information is to put little metal rings on birds' legs. Birds can be ringed in the nest when young, or trapped when older, ringed, and released. If they are trapped again elsewhere, or found dead, the information is sent to central collecting points. Some birds now wear transmitters tracked by satellites.

RAPTOR HOMES DEMOLISHED
The world's rain forests are being chopped down at a fast rate, destroying the homes and habitats of many raptors, and of many other living creatures, all irreplaceable. Habitat loss is the worst of all the problems affecting raptors, and a number of species, such as the Madagascar fish eagle, are close to extinction. Pollution is the second greatest problem, especially in countries where DDT and other long-lasting lethal pesticides are still in use.

Raptor records

THE FASTEST BIRD in the world, the bird with the greatest wing area, the bird that catches the largest quarry – all these are birds of prey. Fossil remains tell us of other remarkable raptors. The plains of Argentina hold the bones of a prehistoric condor-like bird that had an 8-m (25-ft) wingspan. In the recent past there was a species of eagle in New Zealand, Haast's eagle, that was one-third bigger than any living raptor. It only became extinct within the last thousand years. Many of today's most magnificent raptors may join it soon, thanks to human beings. They are in danger because of the damage we cause to the environment, damage which is increasingly rebounding on us. As one scientist said, "An environment unfit for raptors is an environment unfit for humanity."

SPEED KING
The gyrfalcon is the fastest of all the falcons in level flight. It may be the fastest in a stoop as well, because it is the largest and heaviest falcon. The high-speed tests done so far, however, have been on peregrines, so the highest recorded speeds are of peregrines.

LOFTIEST OF THEM ALL
Most birds do not fly very high. They stay low, near their prey. Some, however, do go very high when migrating. Broad-winged hawks go up to 5,000–6,400 m (16,500–20,000 ft). One Rüppell's griffon (above) hit a plane at 10,000 m (37,000 ft) above West Africa, but why this bird was flying so high is a mystery, as Rüppell's griffons do not migrate.

Falcons fold their wings in further than this when stooping really fast

WINGED LIGHTNING
When falcons stoop (dive) down on their prey, they travel faster than any other birds on earth. The peregrine falcon (left) is usually quoted as the fastest, but the other large falcons can probably stoop as fast. The maximum speed of a stoop is disputed. It is probably about 225 km/h (140 mph), although some estimates are higher.

LIVES ANYWHERE, EATS ANYTHING
The black kite is possibly the most common bird of prey in the world. A very adaptable bird, one of the keys to its success is that it will eat almost anything, from fish to the leftovers it finds on rubbish tips. Another is that it lives happily alongside humans. So do American and European kestrels, black vultures, and turkey vultures, also among the most populous raptors in the world.

Black kites have the forked tails typical of kites

Labrador is included to show how big the condor's wings are

A small but genuine raptor

PYGMY RAPTOR
The smallest birds of prey are the seven species of falconet, or pygmy falcon. Despite their size, they look just like the other birds of prey, on a smaller scale. They catch insects, lizards, and even birds nearly as big as they are. The African pygmy falcon (above) is one of the smallest. The very smallest is the black-thighed falconet, which weighs 28–55 g (1–2 oz), and is 14–17 cm (5.5–7 in) high.

GIANT OF THE SKIES
The 3-m (10-ft) wingspan of the Andean condor is second in size only to that of the albatross. The condor's very broad wings give it the greatest wing area of any bird. It needs the wing area to lift it when it flies, because it can weigh up to 13.5 kg (30 lb). The condor is also probably the longest-lived of all the raptors: one condor was brought to the Moscow zoo as an adult (at least five years old) in 1892, and died there in 1964, when it must have been at least 77 years old. No bird in the wild would live anything like that long, but life expectancy generally increases with size among raptors, so condors probably do live the longest.

BACK FROM THE BRINK
At this moment in time, the Californian condor is probably the rarest bird of prey in the world. In the 1980s, shooting, habitat destruction, lead poisoning, and other causes brought the species to a point where there were only 27 birds left, and finally the last wild condors were brought into captivity for their own protection. Fortunately, they breed well in captivity, and they are now being re-released into the wild.

Californian condors are famously ugly

Imperial eagles have special protection, but still may not survive

The white feathers on the back distinguish the imperial eagle from the much more common golden eagle

A forest eagle, the harpy has relatively short, broad wings and a long tail

FATAL FEET
Harpy eagles are probably the most powerful of all raptors. They live in the rainforests of South America and hunt quarry as large as sloths and big monkeys. Female harpy eagles have talon-spans (from front to hind talon) of 20–23 cm (8–9 in). Their hind talons are up to 9 cm (3.5 in) long, bigger than the claws of a grizzly bear.

RAPTORS UNDER PRESSURE
A number of raptor species are endangered. One is the Spanish, or western, species of imperial eagle (above). The total population is probably down to 150 pairs. The causes of its decline include poisoning, a fall in the number of rabbits, and electrocution on power lines. A captive breeding programme has been set up, but has a long way to go. Around the world, habitat destruction is the greatest single problem facing birds of prey, especially for raptors on islands, where the original population is often very small, and the birds have nowhere else to go.

Bird can withdraw its neck into ruff to keep warm

Andean condors have to run to get airborne on flat areas; they prefer to jump off a cliff or run downhill

The largest primary flight feathers in the world

Index

Acknowledgements

Dorling Kindersley would like to thank:
Everyone at the National Birds of Prey Centre, near Newent, Gloucestershire, England (Craig Astbury, John Crooks, Monica Garner, Ian Gibbons, Debbie Grant, Breeze Hale, Angie Hill, Philip Jones, Kirsty Large, Mark Parker, Mark Rich, Jan Stringer).
The Booth Natural History Museum, Brighton (Jeremy Adams); Dr Steve Parry.
Research and editorial assistance:
Sean Stancioff
Design assistance:
Julie Ferris, Iain Morris
Artwork: Bill Le Fever, Gilly

Newman, John Woodcock
Endpapers: Iain Morris
Index: Marion Dent
Additional photography:
Steve Gorton, Alex Wilson, C Laubscher
Picture credits
The publisher would like to thank the following for their kind permission to reproduce the images. t=top, b=bottom, c=centre, l=left, r=right
Ardea, London: Eric Dragesco 24tl.
British Museum: Front Cover tl, Back Cover tl, 50tr, 52tr/53tl.
Bruce Coleman Collection: Jane Burton 49bl, Raimund Cramm 38bl, Peter Davey 58tr, Francisco J. Erize

12bc, Pekka Helo 43tr, Gordon Langsbury 36tl, Mary Plage 27tl, Marie Read 44crb, N. Schwiatz 34cl, Uwe Walz 42br, Joseph Van Warmer 59tl, Staffan Widstrand 16br, Rod Williams 13tl.
Cornell Laboratory of Ornithology, New York: L. Page Brown 38tl.
Dover Publications: 10cra, 13cla, 32tl, 34c, 58tl. **Mary Evans Picture Library:** 40cl, 42tl, 43cl, 45tr, 46tr, 53br, 54tl, Back cover cr. **Frank Lane Picture Agency:** John Hawkins 39bc, E & D Hosking 56 bc, Alan Parker 47tr. **Giraudon, Paris:** 27cb, Avec Authorisation speciale de la Ville De Bayeux 52bl, 52tl.
Robert Harding Picture Library: Photri inc. 36cr. **Hawk Mountain Sanctuary Association, PA, USA:** Wendy Scott 57cr. **Peter Newark's**

Pictures: 42clb. **NHPA:** Martin Wendler 57br, Alan Williams 58cr.
Jemima Parry-Jones: 11tl, 38bc, 40tl, 45crb, 58br, Miguel Lopez 41tl. **Planet Earth:** D. Robert Franz 37tl, Nick Garbutt 47cla, William S. Paton 47tl, David A Ponton 10cl, Mike Read 49tr, Ronald S. Rogoff 43tc, Johnathan Scott 44tc, 44clb, Anup Shah 58cl.
Kati Poynor: 35tl.
RSPB: M. W. Richards 36bl.
Frank Spooner Pictures: Gamma/F. Soir 57bl.
Micheal Zabé: 53tc.
Every effort has been made to trace the copyright holders. Dorling Kindersley apologizes for any unintentional omissions and would be pleased, in such cases, to add an acknowledgement in future editions.